MARKETING

In 1969, after a conspicuously successful career in marketing in industry, John Stapleton established his own marketing consultancy, specialising in research, planning and strategy. He first joined the Institute of Marketing as a student in 1961 and was awarded its Diploma, with distinction, in 1965. The former Honorary Secretary of the Kent Group, he is a member of the Institute's Speakers' Panel and has lectured regularly on marketing at polytechnic colleges in the London area. He is a regular contributor to the management press and the author of several other books on marketing and planning. A graduate of the University of Aston, John Stapleton has compiled the marketing courses for a well-known correspondence college and is at present a lecturer in the Department of Marketing and Advertising at the College for Distributive Trades in London. He is married with two children.

TEACH YOURSELF BOOKS

MARKETING

John Stapleton
D.B.A., Dip.M.Inst.M.

TEACH YOURSELF BOOKS
Hodder and Stoughton

First printed 1975
Third impression 1977

Copyright © 1975
John Stapleton

ISBN 0 340 05967 2

Printed in Great Britain
for Hodder and Stoughton Paperbacks,
a division of Hodder and Stoughton Ltd,
Mill Road, Dunton Green, Sevenoaks, Kent
(Editorial Office: 47 Bedford Square, London WC1 3DP),
by Hazell Watson & Viney Ltd, Aylesbury, Bucks

Contents

Foreword

When my old friend John Stapleton asked me to contribute these few words of commendation, I was delighted to agree. Having been active for a good many years in an occupation which has exposed me to a great deal of writing on marketing, it is a real pleasure, and a privilege, to welcome the appearance of so comprehensive a treatment.

What is so particularly valuable in this book, which will be read by many people with little previous appreciation of the scope and meaning of modern marketing, is the emphasis it places throughout on the importance of planning the activity with preconceived objectives in mind. So much marketing instruction has tended to be sterile, as if employment of marketing technique could, in itself, work the miracle of turning a badly planned and executed operation into a success.

The author's treatment thoroughly reveals the developing complexity of the modern marketing process without at any time becoming pedestrian or unduly demanding. What it achieves in this way is a very clear exposition of why marketing has to be studied, why standards of requirement are rising and why this is a task of nationally important dimensions. Having regard to the many technological and social developments in the rapidly changing world of today, it is to be hoped that many readers will imbibe freely of the treasures within. They will certainly benefit from such a beginning, and I believe those practitioners who have grown up in the hard school of experience will also find the content a very timely reminder of the formal significance marketing is once again acquiring in the world.

E. J. Jenner
Director of Diploma Studies
Institute of Marketing

Preface

Ten years ago the number of marketing books written by British authors could be counted on the fingers of one hand. Now two or three titles are being published each week. Many of these are valuable treatises on particular aspects of marketing and are worthwhile contributions to the body of marketing knowledge and practice. Yet there is a real need for a book of marketing principles and practices which provides a realistic balance between the different activities of marketing. This is the objective behind this Teach Yourself Marketing book. It aims to show that each element in marketing is a highly specialised practice requiring much study effort for a high level of skills to be obtained. It also aims to provide the student, whether he be an established practising manager or a manager of the future, with a concise yet fully explanatory guide to the fundamentals of marketing management.

No marketing practitioner could reach a position of marketing eminence without owing much to colleagues and friends during his career. In my own case I have been fortunate in this respect and am indebted to countless individuals who have contributed to my own development. In particular I must mention Peter Blood, Ted Jenner, Bill Hinder and Charles Dudenay at the Institute of Marketing, Gilbert Cunningham of Morgan Adhesives of Canada, Donald Ingleton of Special Interest Publications, Peter Hopwood of The College for Distributive Trades, Roy Jenkins of Quantum Sciences Ltd, John Winkler of Winkler Marketing Communications Ltd, Owen Palmer of City of London Polytechnic, Mark Maley of Ayala

Designs Ltd, David Roberts of Barnett & Foster Ltd, Peter Harvey of MiA Ltd, Rex Thorne of STC and ITT, Sir John Trelawney, Bart., of Martin Walter (UK) Ltd, and Eric Glover of the Institute of Bankers.

I owe much debt also to my friends and tutors at the University of Aston Management Centre, in particular Joe Smith, Rob Harrison and John Berridge, together with fellow students George A. Poulter, Ted Tedman, Robert Randall, and U Maw Than.

I must also express my appreciation and gratitude to Mr L. B. Curzon, Principal of The College for Distributive Trades, and to the Inner London Education Authority for permission to reproduce from CDT Prospectus the details contained in 12, Marketing as a Career.

I owe my gratitude to the understanding of Mr R. C. Viney, Manager of the National Westminster Bank at Tonbridge, who gave and continues to give exceptional foresight in the interpretation of my financial affairs.

There is also a considerable debt I owe to J. S. Webber of Staflex International Ltd, who read the first draft of this book and added much valuable guidance and comment to the final version.

Finally, I give my heartfelt thanks to my wife, friend, and business partner, Eileen Stapleton, for her inspiration and unstinting devotion to my career and to this book in particular, where as a discriminating consumer, adviser, and typist she has brought the first glimmerings of an idea to the realised work.

The views on education expressed in the text are not intended to represent in any way whatsoever the views of my employers, the Inner London Education Authority.

John Stapleton
June 1974

1 Introduction to Marketing

Successful marketing actions are the result of management information and of applied common sense. Prosperous marketing companies are those that think positively about their business environment, so developing an organisation capable of seeking opportunity, recognising potential and resolving its difficulties. Although marketing techniques are still developing they are becoming increasingly scientific. The artistic qualities once attributed to marketing, mainly by uncomprehending practitioners, are decreasing rapidly in significance and recognition. In many ways this is unfortunate, as much of the inspiration for marketing has come from individual flair.

The word marketing is often equated with what was once called *sales management* but which, since the development of trading, has been known as *distribution*. 'Marketing' is not a synonym for these terms but denotes the wider understanding and greater complexity which have become common in recent years. Before the Industrial Revolution tradesmen produced goods in small quantities for sale in their own close-knit communities. With the increasing availability of machinery it became possible, and indeed necessary, to increase production to pay for the cost of the equipment. Local demand was limited and, although there was some stimulation, it became necessary for the tradesmen to travel to other communities in search of orders.

Constant development and improvement of manufacturing processes has made even larger markets necessary. As markets have grown and production increased, the unit cost of each item manufactured has declined in real terms. Whereas there was a time when only wealthy people could afford most commodities, the reduction in unit cost and increased earnings by operatives have resulted in more and more being bought by the greater part of the population. Effectively, even local markets have shown considerable expansion.

During most of this early industrial period there was no way by which the customer could identify the manufacturer. He would select the goods he required according to his own knowledge and experience. Many goods made available by unscrupulous tradesmen were of a low standard and, in an effort to protect the growth of their industry, suppliers began to put their own names on the goods they produced, indicating to the public that the goods bearing their name would be of an acceptable quality and good value for money. With branding established, manufacturers and tradesmen realised the opportunities for promoting the sale of their own products. Thus publicity and selling techniques, as we know them today, were developed.

Immediately after the end of the Second World War consumer demand was almost insatiable. After many years of being deprived of many of the necessities and comforts of life the public was eager to obtain whatever products it could find. For several years almost every article produced could have been sold many times over. During this period promotional techniques were almost unnecessary. They were only used as a means of informing the public that the manufacturer's goods were now available and where they could be obtained. Gradually this sellers' market eased and firms that had enjoyed constant pressure of demand found that not only were alternative sources of supply established but also consumers were becoming more discriminating in their choice. Quality standards had to be improved. As more and more consumers' demands were satisfied, manufacturers found that they had to develop new markets in order to survive. Once again it became necessary to stimulate demand, not only overseas but also to expand the total market at home.

Faced with a discerning market, manufacturers raised quality standards, redesigned or reformulated products to meet more discriminating tastes, raised the standard of informative literature and emphasised the tangible benefits that their product had over their competitors'. They made it convenient for consumers to purchase by improving distribution facilities and providing satisfactory after-sales service. The need for marketing techniques had returned.

Many non-marketing executives question the validity of marketing expenditure. Marketing activities are the creative element of business activity. They are the means by which the company's income is obtained. They are an integral part of the business and should be considered as much a part of the cost of supply as the productive process itself. Without marketing expenditure there would be no sales; production would be unnecessary. Marketing expenditure for most businesses results in a level of pricing that could not be achieved without modern marketing techniques.

Machine-made shoes conforming to popular taste are made by the thousand at a production cost that may be only a few pence. In making the shoes available in the quantities demanded, the manufacturer is obliged to contribute towards the operating costs and the profit of a wholesaler, who in turn distributes the shoes to retailers, who will also incur operating costs and need to make a profit. Under such circumstances the distribution costs may seem out of all proportion to the manufacturing costs. By comparison, a pair of hand-made shoes selling at, perhaps, two or three times the price of machine-made shoes will have high production costs and distribution costs may be small—just sufficient to pay for the shop at which the cobbler works. In most cases the machine-made shoes will appear to be better value for money to the vast majority of consumers. The purchaser of hand-made shoes will have some special requirement for which he is prepared to pay a higher price. In comparing the two, the marketing costs of machine-made shoes are justified by the effect they have had on the final selling price. Certainly as far as the consumer is concerned, the division between manufacturing and marketing is of little consequence so long as the final price is low.

Distribution costs have also increased as a direct wish of the consumer expressed through demand in the market place. Consumers have shown themselves willing to pay premium prices for products that carry *added value* in convenience. Frozen foods and packaged goods provide this added convenience and consumers pay the additional charges incurred in distributing these goods. Previously consumers had to pay for these processes—not in money but in the time spent in preparing the products for consumption. Many costs of distribution borne by industry are eventually paid for by the consumer to ensure that he or she maintains a freedom of choice, a freedom to buy on credit and the freedom that comes as a result of the educational efforts made by industry and commerce.

Part of the marketing process is devoted to reducing the cost of other marketing activities and to avoiding production waste; research for example, into channels and costs of distribution, promotional techniques and particularly development of products that consumers need. Henry Ford has long been acclaimed a pioneer of mass production. Yet it is clear from his autobiography that he was also a pioneer of the modern marketing philosophy. In *My Life and Work* he tells how he first found the price at which cars would sell by the million, then developed his production techniques accordingly. So by carrying out market research, he was helping to reduce production costs of cars. Research into consumer needs may also result in a change in the presentation of products from their natural form. The orange has been available for thousands of years, but in recent times marketing men have changed its shape and its constitution in order to make it more acceptable to consumers. At one time in the past an enterprising entrepreneur considered whether people would prefer, say, as an extreme example, a square orange. While considering the shape of the fruit he decided that having to peel off the skin and eliminate the pips was not only time-consuming but also left the eater's fingers undesirably sticky. He also decided that the sharp taste was not to everyone's liking and that the product should be sweetened. In developing all these factors he produced orange squash and made it available in a bottle. Today the process has gone even further in the evolutionary cycle and the juice of the orange is now available chilled or frozen in a concentrated form.

Concepts in marketing

In order to understand marketing principles the non-marketing executive must become accustomed to entirely new concepts. To the professional marketer products are not just what they are but what they do. 'Selling the sizzle not the steak' is an expression frequently used to denote marketing theory. In persuading a consumer to buy a product for which a latent need has been established, a marketing-orientated company presents its goods in a way that will appeal to the consumers' needs. In emphasising benefits to the consumer, the seller is portraying his product in its best possible light and is helping the potential buyer to understand what the product will do for him; for example, in promoting a brand of petrol, the seller recognises the need for economical motoring and will emphasise the mileage that may be achieved through using his product. Other sellers may believe that the consumer is more interested in buying a product that not only fulfils its main purpose but will also satisfy psychological needs. The cosmetic manufacturer or the dressmaker will often concentrate promotional themes on the beauty the user can obtain in the same way that the pharmaceutical manufacturer will stress the health-giving qualities of his product—for both product groups help to instil confidence and hope in the user and so give him or her greater satisfaction from life. Equally, the industrial manufacturer may promote the idea of reduced worry rather than emphasise the increased efficiency that may be possible.

Although often described as a promotional or a distributive activity, marketing is a function whose ultimate aim is to maximise profitability. It can best be described as a fundamental policy-forming activity devoted to selecting and developing suitable products for sale—promoting and distributing these products in a manner providing the optimum return on capital employed. As the optimum rate of profitability is usually achieved through high production runs, the greater the numbers of a particular product produced, the better the profit opportunity. In essence this means manufacturing the product that is likely to appeal to the majority of the population. The consumer still retains freedom of choice because smaller firms will concentrate their efforts on gaps left by the larger companies. Often the larger company will provide a wide choice by producing a basic product and providing many optional extras sufficient to appeal to the most extreme tastes. Although breadth of choice is still reduced, variety will always be maintained dependent upon demand. In this way choice is decided by the market.

The growth of marketing techniques in the twentieth century has been aided by parallel advances in international communications. International travel, worldwide tourism and the speed at which persons can move from one part of the world to another have created a 'shrinkage' in the size of the globe. Social, cultural and nationalistic barriers are being eliminated. The telephone, radio, television and space satellites have brought the nations of the world closer to each other—hence the BOAC Earthshrinkers Campaign—with greater understanding and tolerance towards historical differences. Such developments have made it easier for manufacturers to create worldwide mass markets for their products. This easing of communication has made it possible for educational and other influential actions to create a common acceptance for certain products. Bigger markets and increasing demand have required greater capitalisation for production and for the introduction of more economical manufacturing techniques.

The increasing complexity of products available and the ever-growing rate of technological progress have made it difficult for the average consumer to be knowledgeable when buying goods. Manufacturers make use of marketing activities to make available to purchasers the necessary information. Advertising campaigns and descriptive literature are intended to make available the information a consumer requires to decide for himself the product most suitable for his needs. Manufacturers are not expected to be impartial in the information they provide. Each manufacturer has made a product which he feels is most suitable for the market and he will always emphasise the most important features in his promotional activities. He could not—nor could he be expected to—provide information on product qualities which he believes are unnecessary and which he has chosen not to include in his own product. To make a satisfactory purchase the consumer must obtain information from competing manufacturers and decide for himself which particular products and specific benefits he seeks from the range concerned. Often the consumer will decide in favour of a well-known and well-established manufacturer in whom he is able to place some confidence because of the company's name and past reputation. He may make this decision irrespective of the competing values of the products concerned. Consumer organisations such as the Consumers Association, the publishers of *Which*, help in this process by accelerating the effect that differentials in the market place would achieve.

Although many people still dispute the validity of marketing practices in a business enterprise, it is reasonable to assume that a wise businessman would not make continually increasing investment in marketing unless he were convinced that he was getting value for money. Marketing activities are not yet exactly quantifiable, but more and more efforts are being made to develop marketing into a more exact science. At this stage it is possible to apply logical deductions by observation, in a general assessment of marketing effectiveness. By carefully assembling market information, management is able to reduce business risk by the elimination of non-influencing data, thus improving general economic prosperity. Planning future requirements carefully in each stage of the distribution process enables a company to avoid unnecessary expenditure in mis- directed and ineffective investment. By setting sales targets and developing marketing strategy to achieve these targets the company creates effective new markets among existing and new customers. Developing better understanding of customer needs enables a company to improve its communication pro- cesses. It can provide better information and services for these customers, thus creating additional goodwill among the many organisations involved in its day-to-day operations.

In any business environment there will always be an infinite number of variables which are often in conflict. Applied marketing techniques help to reduce the number of such variables and to channel company resources towards maximising profits and minimising costs according to short-, medium- or long-term needs. In the struggle to win more profitable sales a company may make use of a wide variety of specialist skills. It is in selecting and co-ordinating these skills that the marketing function is seen to perform its most obvious function. The marketing mix, as this permutation is known, is based on the requirements in the market place, provided that these needs are sufficient in volume to attract the attention of the company concerned.

Definitions of marketing

Numerous definitions of marketing have been suggested by any number of learned authorities, companies and writers. In some cases the emphasis has been on the concept of marketing. in others on the activities of marketing. It is clear that the two are inter-dependent, yet where the concept is understood the activities are a natural consequence. Where the concept is not understood, then the activities may be misdirected and ineffective.

Some companies may indicate that despite the non-existence of a marketing department they have still been successful. This does not mean that the company has not been marketing orientated, for the executives concerned may be fully aware of the concept of marketing and may practise its principles without giving title to the functions involved. It is, however, unfortunately still common for a company to appoint marketing executives and yet not understand the basic requirements of the marketing function. Certainly the activities of marketing seem clear, for they will normally include the promotional activities of the company along with the required ancillary services. The marketing concept is less definite but more fundamental to business success. It is a management philosophy, an attitude of mind, to which the complete involvement of every company executive and employee is necessary, and in which the entire operation of the company is devoted towards the satisfaction of consumer needs. The definition adopted by the Institute of Marketing is as follows:

'Marketing is the management function which organises and directs all those business activities involved in assessing and converting customer purchasing power into effective demand for a specific product or service, and in moving the product or service to the final consumer or user so as to achieve the profit target or other objective set by the company.'

There is no doubt from this definition that the Institute clearly recognises the management philosophy of marketing and that successful companies are those that adopt this philosophy at all levels. In a modern company no functional executive, or white- or blue-collar worker, is without some direct or indirect contact with the firm's markets. The attitudes of the chief executive will be communicated via the staff to customers. The floor sweeper in the factory will have an effect on the customers in the way that he performs his tasks in keeping dust from, say, precision machinery or food vats. Every employee in searching for a new job is conveying impressions of his employers to everyone who sees him and has a need for his particular skill. No individual in today's company should, therefore, lack motivation in marketing understanding.

In normal circumstances the primary contact which management takes as priority is with customers. Not only is this concept critical but even the practice of marketing involves other functional activities, for all commercial functions have some sort of customer contact. It is for this reason that marketing direction overlaps into other business functions.

The entrepreneur in marketing

All commercial activities are created to provide goods or services. During their evolution many firms expand their activities, often with new products and new markets. At the time of creation the entrepreneur usually tries to meet an existing need rather than to stimulate a new demand or highlight an unconscious one.

Normally he will have established connections, a specific skill or knowledge and an awareness of the requirements of his potential customers. At this time his business activity is probably clear and he is unlikely to have felt the need to consider fully the scope of his operations or to formulate his operational problems in depth. But this is not always the case where the entrepreneur concerned has already had extensive managerial experience. An example from industry is provided by Midcast Numerical Control (Wales) Ltd. The present Managing Director, Jim Davies, saw a requirement for an expert organisation totally committed to the application of numerical control systems. So in the mid-1960s he set up a team operating in small premises in Leicester where he had daily access to any part of the country and where there was an abundance of skilled engineering labour. His company and its associates are pioneers of the use of numerical control as the technological Esperanto of Europe, since numerical control dismisses the main difficulty of international collaboration—the language barrier among engineers and technicians.

In the industry facing Midcast the ideal marketing pitch is technical competence. So the company saw its opportunity, knew its market and, because it had always kept its finger on the pulse, was able to organise almost from the start the full range of services, a programming package, necessary for sound growth. Now based in South Wales, the company operates a twenty-four hour shift. In 1972 it was given a BNEC Export Award in recognition of overseas sales, which, from a few hundred pounds in 1969, had reached £250 000 by March 1971 and £1 million by mid-1972. Each step of the way had been preset and organised according to best management practice.

Established companies, on the other hand, operating in a mixture of growing, static or declining markets, and who need to reappraise their business functions regularly and to assess their future prospects for survival, regrettably do not seem to practise the same discipline. Often failure to do so may result in lost market share, product obsolescence, redundancies or even bankruptcy.

Acceptance of marketing principles and the use of marketing techniques have sometimes been forced on companies by competitive pressures in the market place. In an effort to stimulate demand for their own brands, manufacturers seek product innovation and attempt to improve the effectiveness of their operations by researching and developing the needs of consumers. Industrial companies have been slower to adopt marketing techniques, for their production, in unit terms, has been relatively small and their number of customers comparatively low. They do not often achieve a dominant market share and any contraction in immediate purchasing levels is spread evenly over the larger part of the market. Industrial companies also tend to be more widely diversified in their product range, and a depression in one industry may be compensated in another. Because of their size such companies tend to be more flexible and can adjust to lower production rates more readily.

One could well argue that the adoption of marketing techniques by industrial companies has been forced on them by stagnant national economies and competition from the whole of manufacturing industry for the limited capital investment available. In this sense typewriters are competing against computers for the industrial buyers' money.

Service industries

Few of the service industries have yet felt the pressure of competitive forces with sufficient intensity for the practice of marketing to have been widely adopted. True, retail stores are more market conscious now that other methods of serving the customer have been developed. In the insurance market, companies have had to become market orientated. Traditionally a selling operation, insurance companies have had to develop more sophisticated selling techniques and to look at the problems of the buyer. The emphasis is now on insurance as a savings medium, due to income tax advantages, rather than as a security arrangement. Once again marketing adoption has come from competition—from unit trusts. The competition has forced a substantial increase in the total market, a frequent result of marketing usage.

Until the breakdown of the tariff agreement between insurance companies, active competition was restricted. It is such restrictive practices that have delayed the development of marketing techniques in many service industries. These contain a large element of professional men practising rules of conduct imposed by collective agreement among members of the appropriate association. There are over 150 such professional bodies, with hundreds of thousands of members.

Members may not be allowed to advertise, they are often forbidden to obtain business by pricing concessions, and they must not endeavour to sell or promote their business in the generally accepted way. The sole means by which they expect to win new business is by recommendation. Professional bodies believe that these agreements are in the public interest and that they help to maintain minimum standards of competence.

The United Kingdom's Monopolies Commission in its 1970 report did not agree. The Comission said that the agreements were a restraint on the improvement of efficiency and tended to protect the incompetent. The Commission recommended the abolition of all such restrictive practices, leaving the way clear for the introduction of marketing activities by the more progressive organisations.

The banking profession has suffered at the hands of successive governments through restrictions on the use of its basic product—by squeeze and by freeze. In return for the co-operation of the banking movement Parliament produced its own banking-type operation—the National Giro—and then allowed it advantages that had been withheld from the banking system. In facing this competition and in overcoming the restrictions to growth from which it had suffered for so long, the banking profession adopted marketing attitudes and practices at a speed that would delight many a hardened marketing protagonist. In consequence, the National Giro in facing the new initiative has failed to achieve its original objectives.

International marketing

Competition at home has forced many companies to search overseas for outlets. In order to exploit the best of its opportunities, the forward-looking company will increase its sales abroad so as to maximise profit potential. Modern management does not operate in an atmosphere conducive to selling internationally—or so it seems. This attitude is inconsistent with the concept of marketing, which does not differentiate between groups of people by region. Markets are divided by need or by application of a product which satisfies that need. Marketing opportunities exist wherever there are people, and the fact that these people may be separated by political, cultural or social differences does not necessarily diminish the degree of opportunity. These differences may only influence the way in which the opportunity is seized.

It is necessary first to evaluate the existing opportunities and then to plan to satisfy those showing signs of producing the best results. By assessing the most common needs throughout the globe, and in particular those indicating a future substantial growth rate, and by developing the product which best satisfies that need, the company will not only be adopting the best current marketing practice but will also be well on the way to successful overseas development.

Principles of marketing

An understanding of the true nature of marketing has been shown by Roy Jenkins, managing director of Quantum Sciences Ltd, who explains:

'At one extreme end of marketing-orientated units is the market-orientated company. Such an organisation sets up a selling machine designed to operate in one or more clearly defined market places. It operates by feeding to this machine products of any description which can be sold economically in the chosen markets. It maximises the efficiency of the selling machine by multiplying the opportunities to make sales from a wide product range without significantly increasing calling or other costs. The market-orientated company accepts no short term flexibility in choice of the market but complete flexibility in terms of supply.

'At the other extreme is the product or production-orientated company. It is usual to think of this type of organisation as being the opposite of marketing-orientated but this is not necessarily so. This sort of unit can still use marketing techniques.

'The product or production-orientated organisation is tied by materials or technical equipment or people to a narrow band of products. Whatever field it operates in it is essentially a "quarry". It cannot profitably move on to a new "hole" until it has earned enough profits to be able to abandon the old one. However, it does have complete flexibility in its choice of markets and selling methods. The move of the brewers into production of antibiotics is an obvious example of the utilisation of existing production methods to match the needs of a new market. Most of the famous names in fine china with large investments in clay mines and plant are now earning the bulk of their profits from industrial ceramics. In the early 1950s the author took a small photographic and block-making outfit and moved into the new field of electronics printed production without spending a penny on new plant.'

Often the framework within which the company decides to operate comes as a result of segmentation, or gap-analysis as it is often termed. The process of segmentation may be through markets, products or even geographical areas. Usually the term is associated with markets. Spotting a gap in a market, seeing a need and providing the means by which that need is satisfied portrays the commonly accepted version of the marketing entrepreneur. And it is this vision—sighting an opportunity, seizing it and devoting one's entire existence to its success—that is the predominant feature of market segmentation. Such an example is provided by Norman Fletcher (Sales and Developments) Ltd of Burntwood, Staffs.

In 1960 Norman Fletcher, a West Bromwich shop-owner and life-long boating enthusiast, set about designing a boat.

He was dissatisfied with the performance of the small runabout he owned at the time. After much trial and error and long exhaustive evenings he finally developed his own glass-fibre design. Being full of his own achievement he wasted no time in putting it to the ultimate test—on the water. It attracted much immediate attention and comment. Knowing the boating fraternity well, he backed his own judgment and began manufacturing replicas on a small scale. Soon after he sold a boat to Ray Potter, a notable racing enthusiast, who promptly expressed his satisfaction in his new acquisition by offering to join Norman in his enterprise. *They both knew that crowded roads were frustrating people's drive for speed and excitement. The comparative safety of boat and sea, and the tranquillity away from crowds were bound to catch on.* In 1972 the company was chasing a sales turnover approaching £1 million. During that year it was awarded a BNEC Award for export performance. And yet the product life cycle has only just begun.

An example of product segmentation is given by Morgan Adhesives of Canada, where through advanced technology the company has developed adhesives suitable for pressure application with paper, foils and vinyls. Using this highly flexible and multi-purpose product the company has been able to develop business applications for use in a wide range of industries.

For geographical segmentation we can consider the Fife Forge Co. Ltd of Kirkcaldy in Scotland. Although 100 years old the company made a major change in its policy in 1963, when it began the gradual introduction of a young management team, revised its entire marketing strategy and developed a modernisation programme for its production facilities. The gradual decline of the shipbuilding industry in the UK required the company to seek markets elsewhere. The new management team decided to explore opportunities in markets, especially in the underdeveloped countries, where indigenous forges did not exist. By carrying out market research into the world shipbuilding industry, several likely countries were selected and in-depth investigations were started to establish the requirements in each particular country. Considerable determination was required, for it was five years before results began to accrue favourably. But from 1968 onwards the effort showed increasing rewards. The sales turnover doubled during the period and a loss of £6000 in 1963 was transformed into a profit of £111 000 in 1971, during which year the company was honoured with a BNEC Award for its export achievements. A Queen's Award followed in 1972. The company succeeded by selecting geographical market segments.

Many manufacturers make the mistake of trying to offer a full range for a particular model in a new market. This may work for a car manufacturer, where servicing facilities are critical to sales, but usually it is more practical to enter the market with one product showing promise, establish the company's name among consumers and distributors, and later widen the range as the demand justifies. Apart from the ease with which agents become better acquainted with one product, the marketing effort can be more concentrated.

If a marketing man accepts the principle that there is scope in any business depending on the way he goes about it, and studies his market, his product and his operational methods, he will probably find that he has become a pioneer in his industry. The most startling innovations have come from men who have looked at industries operating without significant change over many years and who plugged the gaps they found.

Distribution and marketing

Frequently traditional business practices work against the newcomer. Competing on equal terms is often impossible. Established companies not only have the confidence of the trade but, in order to protect their vested interests, they may often make deliberate efforts to deter new entrants. One of the major justifications for the massive advertising campaigns between the detergents giants was to make it impossible for other companies to break into the market.

For this reason supermarkets are pressing the own-label product because it induces outlet loyalty rather than the brand loyalty being built by manufacturers.

Sometimes the trade will oppose a new product, no matter how superior it may be, unless the promoter can advertise at a level that will ensure sales exceeding those of the existing product. Often the companies that try innovation stimulate the total market and a more substantial market results—to the benefit of all.

2 The Practice of Marketing

In a modern emancipated society the individual is allowed a measure of free will and choice and is allowed to make his own decisions, whether they be right or wrong for him. In allowing these freedoms there must be competition for his preferences, and a drive for resultant profits is tolerable. This is the basis upon which our society lives and expands.

It contrasts with a totalitarian state operating a planned economy, where some official decides on behalf of the population what its tastes should be, what is good for it and how it should spend its money. In such a society there is no universal demand for marketing practices, although some of its activities exist in other forms, such as propaganda.

Marketing is an integral part of the business operation. It is the fundamental by which industry sells its products. To curtail marketing or to eliminate it altogether would be like suggesting that industry should stop selling—a process that would remove the dynamic element in the national economy and hence diminish the growth rate in both production and job opportunity. In some industries, such as office equipment or data processing, it would be more than the growth rate that would suffer. In the new industries, selling to new markets is essential, and in the modernised production plants of the established industries marketing effort is necessary to achieve the volume essential in maintaining low unit costs and remaining competitive internationally. So marketing provides the stimulus upon which economic progress is based. Without it modern industry tends to stagnate, for it is marketing practice that makes improvements in productivity possible and so gives society the improved standard of living it constantly demands. In the UK during the 1960s and the early 1970s Selective Employment Tax discriminated against the practice of marketing and the Advertising Levy, rejection of a second commercial television channel and closure of private radio stations limited the growth of trade without limiting the growth in production capacity—a dominant feature in the National Plan of 1964. Mass unemployment, high prices and counter industrial action have prevailed. Any possible connection cannot be ignored.

The most criticised activity of marketing is advertising. Salesmanship has always been the subject of dispute, but it is always possible for consumers to take refuge from its practitioners. Not so with advertising, for that is partly the secret of its success. Advertisements appear in the morning mail, on every form of transport, are widespread in leisure pursuits *and follow the family into the home at night via the television screen*; advertising is therefore complementary to selling. There are some who believe the sole purpose of advertising is to inform. This is inaccurate. Advertising is intended to inform in order to sell. It sells by informing people in as persuasive a way as possible. It emphasises the benefits that the manufacturer develops in his product so that the consumer might buy. The advertiser describes his product as being the best there is because he believes this to be true. And it is—for his chosen market. He has spent time researching the market place and establishing people's needs, and has then developed a product accordingly. Following this he goes out into the market place and promotes the product he has specially developed for the market he has selected. For people in that market his product is the best value for money available. So the manufacturer will not normally give information on the limitations inherent in his product or, generally speaking, on applications for which the product is unsuitable. Nor should he be expected to. The features he believes necessary are included and the appropriate applications indicated; anything else has been left out as unwarranted. He cannot be held responsible for the wishful thinking of consumers—the hope that their £1 will buy a product worth £5. So in marketing terms the manufacturer will have selected a group of people as his market, and he provides the appropriate product most suitable for them. He cannot in all fairness be expected to give details of facilities he considers unnecessary and be responsible for and to people for whom the product has not been made. People who accuse manufacturers of misleading practices are often guilty of their own inability or disinclination to study and compare the available alternatives.

How marketing benefits society

Marketing is practised in every country where goods are in abundance. One of the inadequacies of the UK National Plan of 1964 was the emphasis on increasing production as if that were a means of increasing the wealth of the nation. In fact, wealth comes from selling goods, not from simply producing them; ask any businessman left with a warehouse full of unsaleable goods. Equally, any emphasis on increasing productivity is inadequate without a parallel increase in consumption. Producing more goods per worker implies more sales needed per worker and, logically, more consumption to absorb the extra produce. You cannot increase the wealth of the nation without raising consumption and that requires marketing. Production is a poor second, for wealth can be improved *without raising the level of production*. Increasing prices alone will suffice but only in the short term.

The principal benefits of marketing to society are:

1 Lowering of prices
2 Improving quality
3 Reducing business risk
4 Aiding technological progress

5 Subsidising education and leisure
6 Reducing cognitive dissonance
7 Providing jobs
8 Creating consumer choice

These factors all contribute to improving the standard of living of the nation, and in many ways perform the socialistic doctrine of more for everyone. The way in which this is achieved is complex but the philosophy is simple. Consider the factors closely:

1 Lowering of prices

All economists agree on the principle of the economies of scale. Some may question its truth in practice, but all agree that it is possible and often achievable. Certainly the unit-cost price of a product is reduced after mass markets have been opened. Not all achieve dramatic reductions in price, for many reductions are almost indiscernible. Women's tights, prior to mini-skirts, were used generally by entertainers and sports personalities, and a typical good-quality pair retailed at £1.50 a pair. Today's price is as low as 12½p, and tights sell by the million instead of by the thousand. But most products take many years to reach high volume sales and reduction in cost prices are achieved quite slowly. So instead of introducing actual price reductions, manufacturers tend to absorb many cost increases and raise selling prices at a rate much lower than inflation would suggest. Therefore in real terms prices are falling relative to increases in purchasing power.

2 Improving quality

In the earlier part of the century competing goods were largely homogeneous and not distinguishable one from the other. But with the advancement of advertising, manufacturers started to put their name on their product and branding spread. So in competition for the purchasers' money, manufacturers struggled to improve the quality of their output. Sometimes this would be by the reformulation of a product and sometimes by repackaging or even redesigning the product to make it more acceptable. In this way frozen foods or instant mixes are considered improvements in quality.

3 Reducing business risk

Although this may seem primarily to the benefit of the capitalist, it does nonetheless bring considerable benefits to society. Marketing helps to improve the quality of business decisions, and that can mean avoidance of waste of resources and less likelihood of business failure and unemployment.

It also implies more confidence in the taking of risks, and hence the whole of society benefits from the extra product choices thus made available.

4 Aiding technological progress

In the struggle to prosper, or even survive, firms must innovate—not just in commercial practices but in products themselves. It is modern marketing that has enabled products such as Xerography, ballpoint pens, colour television and the like to become readily available to those who want them. Technological progress rarely comes from the scientist working outside commercial pressures. The only commercial technological spin-off from the American space programme was non-stick frying pans. Yet commercially there have been many new ideas, ranging from moon-walk toys to telephone operator mouthpieces.

5 Subsidising education and leisure

Neither the newspaper industry nor commercial television could survive today without marketing subsidies. Newspapers rely on advertising revenue for the larger part of their income, while commercial television is dependent entirely on the advertisers' money. These two media account for the most significant proportion of after-school education, whether it be cultural, academic, scientific, moral, religious, artistic or whatever. Advertisers also support most of the leisure pursuits; because they want to appeal *en masse* they tend to spend their money where people gather together, at sports grounds etc. Furthermore, advertisers support such activities as round the world voyages, beauty competitions and man's flamboyant struggle against the elements. So modern life would be inconceivable without marketing influences.

6   Reducing cognitive dissonance
All buyers are wary of making a mistake, for no one can be an expert on all things. But well-promoted goods offered by well-known companies with such policies as sale on approval, sale or return, or after-sales services provide reassurance. In this way consumers are relieved of anxiety. They will be able to buy relatively expensive items confident of the quality and assured of service and attention should something be wrong.

7   Providing jobs
Higher levels of demand brought by marketing necessitate distribution channels and physical distribution facilities. As such, the infrastructure of the nation involving ports, roads, motorways, ships, trucks, trains, airports, and telecommunication networks becomes critical and the provision of these services brings jobs to millions.

8   Creating consumer choice
Competition and the need to achieve a return on investment compels firms continually to extend their product range. Consumers are provided with a full choice, sufficient to satisfy all but the most difficult tastes.

By the judicial use of its marketing funds, today's company makes it possible for almost everyone to share the fruits of progress. Although the initial, often extravagant quality sometimes suffers, and complaints come most frequently from those able to disregard the price tag, it is considered better for everyone to enjoy a mediocre product mass-produced than for the majority to go without altogether. It would not be extreme to say that improvements in the standard of living achieved this century by advanced nations are largely attributable to marketing and the influence it has had in the allocation of productive resources. One could say almost that capitalism has been achieving the aims of socialism.

The marketing family tree

Marketing is still the subject of much misunderstanding, for it is not just the prodigy of the twentieth century but a whole family of prodigies. The father goes back many centuries to the beginning of trading, when merchants recognised the need to obtain the foods people craved for rather than products that might have been just food for their souls. The mother is a phenomenon of the nineteenth and twentieth centuries. Using the fast-developing network of communication systems, the 'activities of marketing', the so-called marketing mix, joined with the ancient 'concept of marketing' and spawned the family of today. Moreover, it is the confusion in identifying the offspring that antagonises most non-marketing executives. For although they spring from the same seed and believe in the same philosophies, the branches of the marketing family tree have reached different degrees of maturity and, like all children, have formed their own unique characteristics. So the practice of marketing in each branch of the family shows a markedly different profile. The branches are:

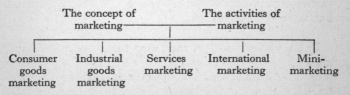

Each of these areas of marketing practice has used the

principle or principles most applicable to its own market—true market orientation, and developed it to the point where it may almost dominate marketing management. Thus in consumer goods marketing, where adequate distribution is sought by the use of *advertising pull*—getting consumers to seek and ask for the product by name—marketing is almost synonymous with advertising; certainly the marketing manager or brand manager will be an advertising man, probably with agency experience. Similarly, in industrial goods marketing, where outlets are comparatively few, the most significant activity is selling—the winning of confidence—and the top marketing job will be filled by a former salesman, almost invariably from the same industry, since established contact is almost invaluable—*sales push*.

Consumer goods marketing

In the early days of established trading practices the manufacturer had to depend on merchants to carry his goods far and wide for sale in provincial or colonial market towns. Bartering was common and dishonesty in trade an accepted practice. Goods were degraded and suppliers paid with debased coin. So in order to prosper and grow a manufacturer had to find a distribution network that gave honesty and reliability. The tied-house system in public houses is probably attributable to this need. Door-to-door selling, as practised by pedlars, was the only alternative to the merchants selling at the village markets, so chaos was assured. The image left by these traders lingers on in society's view of selling and salesmanship.

But the consumer goods industry was rescued, not by the trade channels but by a collection of consumers. For manufacturers were not the only ones to suffer from dishonest traders; the customers themselves resisted any extension of the practice by setting up their own retail outlets with goods manufactured under the control of the retailer—the birth of the co-operative movement. Within ten years the pioneers of

Rochdale launched the Co-operative Wholesale Society, in 1855, to supply the branches that had been opened. By the end of the century multiple traders in the UK, such as Liptons and Home & Colonial, had opened hundreds of branches in competition with the Co-op. So the mass marketing of foods hitherto the province of the affluent, such as flour, tea, sugar and dairy produce, was established, and not by mass communications but by distribution networks that brought goods to the doorstep of the working population. Coming as it did soon after the Industrial Revolution, which had laid the foundations for a successful marketing nation, a growing and prosperous middle class, the marketing of the necessities of life achieved an unheard of velocity.

The non-food producers soon recognised the advantages of establishing their own outlets where quality was assured and a successful sale earned a bonus, goodwill, towards a subsequent sale (a satisfied customer becomes a regular customer). And so the big names of today founded their businesses. Some, such as Boots and Timothy Whites, had been established earlier as pharmaceutical preparation manufacturers. They now wished to sell direct to the public by opening their own branches. Others, such as Marks & Spencer, began as retailers and extended activities into manufacturing later.

Even today mass marketing depends on effective distribution. No amount of advertising can force a sale if the product is not available at the customers' favourite outlet. Furthermore, a good advertising campaign may benefit competitors more than it does the advertiser if their distribution is better. Once interested in the idea of a particular product a consumer will soon try another offered by the retailer if the advertised product is not immediately available.

Nevertheless, mass distribution is difficult to achieve today without the support of an extensive promotional campaign. Retailers are faced with so many alternatives that they must discriminate in favour of those that will sell well and advertising, particularly on television, helps to achieve that objective. So selling to retailers must be accompanied by the promise of extensive promotional support.

Advertising as we know it today became possible following the advancement of communications. Yet it was dependent on the branding of goods. At one time the grocer stored products in jars or in sacks on the floor. As manufacturers became conscious of the need to provide guarantees of quality standards for their produce, they included their names on the goods. They also tried to make them as attractive as possible to consumers. So branding was introduced and the packaging industry received a stimulus which it believes, even now, is only the start of something big.

But today, even with branding and advertising established, it is still distribution that provides the way to successful consumer goods marketing. Advertising may make distribution channels more effective, but it cannot replace them entirely. Self-service and supermarkets are the major innovation in recent years, followed by mail order, yet another distribution channel. Even so, this twentieth-century revolution in distribution is considered the tip of the iceberg. For future generations, distribution must continue to be the significant element in the marketing mix, with consumer convenience being the major criterion for success, rather than price or even absolute quality standards. So finding the 'convenience' consumers need is the major marketing problem in consumer goods.

Industrial goods marketing

The Americans are often given the credit for establishing marketing practices. This is probably true of consumer goods, largely because the sheer vastness of the country provided the initiating distribution problem, but it is far from true as regards industrial goods. Industrial goods sales rely largely on the use of selling ability, a practical necessity that has been successfully employed by firms in the capital goods industries for longer than advertising has existed. Companies marketing industrial goods have had to create markets where markets did not exist before. Selling a tin of beans requires an identifiable purchaser who pays and reaps benefits. Building a bridge, a dam or a railway line, or installing a telephone network all provide very real benefits, to the entire population of a nation. Yet who pays? So when selling to governments, all of whom have to decide between bread today and jam tomorrow, it is essential to develop infrastructure and so ensure growth in market potential. In this way the capital goods industry is self-perpetuating, yet it must still feed off that growth.

Because of its overseas territories the UK had what amounted to captive markets. Moreover, because these territories needed industrial products in order to advance their own economies, they provided substantial growth and growth potential to the UK. But the country had to solve the problems of physical distribution first. The ox and the horse had been the major means of transport for many centuries, but they were inadequate for widespread and rapid distribution of capital goods. So railway networks, waterways and canals, shipping and port facilities became essential for industrialisation. British-owned, they provided the service factor essential to successful marketing. These investments provided the basis for the wealth of the British nation, and thus British industrial marketing led the world. However, these investments also laid the foundation for the present lack of growth of the country. The British people had too many vested interests to protect and, because of the extent of these interests, departures from traditional use tended to be avoided. Yet in this changing world expediency has become the critical factor in marketing. The British attitude of making one piece of equipment last longer than a lifetime became redundant. Now the life cycle of production machines has become significant. Reliability and long life are not as important as high production rates, flexibility to meet changing market needs, and equipment made at a price designed to bring a shorter life and rapid depreciation. Clearly economies of scale are better realised in new machines, operating at faster rates than would twice as many machines at slower rates. No better example is available than that provided by the British machine tool industry. It once led the world but is now being forced out of its own backyard by Japanese, German and American equipment. So to sell equipment the capital goods industry must sell ideas, and overcoming apathy is its major marketing task. For it must be remembered that all trading depends on consumer consumption. The ultimate aim of all manufacture, whether for the production of consumer goods or the assembly of capital goods needed to produce consumer goods, is to satisfy consumer demand—the source of all monies and purchasing power.

The marketing of professional services

It is perhaps a paradox of modern life that the very area in which marketing has been practised the longest is the one that has acquired a reputation for lack of awareness in modern marketing techniques. It is perhaps because the practice of marketing has so long been a feature of the scene that it is now fully integrated and not easy to identify, or even isolate. That is not to say that all professional services are long established, for clearly many are the result of scientific advances in this century. Hence the need for specialisation—a division of labour in the intellectual sense. It is true, however, that professional services do include the oldest known to man. Unfortunately, in a discussion of the origins of man's activities, good or bad, there is always some sensitivity—perhaps because so many things that are sacred today grew from such dubious beginnings that society does not wish to be reminded of those earlier times. Even so, some practices are frowned upon today, just as they were thousands of years ago. The pursuits 'health, wealth and stealth' are immortal. But we cannot ignore history. The services of the witch-doctor, the alchemist, the prostitute and the money-lender are but the origins of medicine, physics, the theatre and banking. Politics grew out of oppression and slavery, while early religion was based on fear of the unknown and idolatry. But the unique characteristic associated with these early services remains today. They all depend on faith —the psychological acceptance of some future satisfaction— for all provide post-operative effects. This means that marketing evidence must be based on credibility. Decisions as to the use of the service must be made on personal judgment backed by knowledge and experience. And once the service has been used there is no alternative against which it can be measured. For the alternative, not using the service, is liquidated the moment the service is put into operation. In this sense measurement of the value of the service is indeterminate except at an empirical level. Often it becomes pre-service hope followed by post-service justification.

At the time of hiring a professional service the business executive cannot be sure of what he has bought. He feels the expectation that his problem may be overcome. But even then he cannot be sure that what he thinks his problem is will agree with that diagnosed by the professional.

So it will have to depend on trust, and that trust will only be formed when the professional has shown himself capable of understanding the real problems of the client. Winning his confidence is therefore an essential ingredient.

It was suggested earlier that the marketing of professional services had a low profile because the practice of marketing had been fully absorbed into the service provided, mainly in the form of mystique, and so was indistinguishable from the actual facilities offered. This is, of course, a simplification, for many professional services reject, through their elected representatives, all forms of advertising and promotion as being unethical. In the UK the Monopolies Commission rejected the claims made by the professions and implied that they were restrictive practices and not in the public interest. Clearly there is considerable scope for the enterprising. But even so, the practitioner still has an opportunity to further marketing practice without offending his sincere, if out-dated, beliefs. Clean and attractive premises, modern equipment, warmth and comfort, civility from staff, and attention to the true interests of clients could benefit many. Belief in austerity, traditional methods, poor administration and complete disregard for any form of organisation is not the best recipe for overcoming the credibility gap—the marketing problem of the professions.

Marketing internationally

Marketing at an international level in any sophisticated sense is the baby of the marketing family. So far the youngster has used ideas borrowed from its brothers. Its own development seems to be dependent on the final rejection of the now long-established theory of comparative advantages. This theory suggests that a nation should concentrate its efforts on those goods and services that command a high return in export markets and import those that it cannot produce itself or for which it cannot compete on production costs. The disadvantage of this theory is that it assumes a more or less equal distribution of 'wealth' and a continuing demand for each type of goods and services compatible with the needs and aspirations, at any one time, of the nations so endowed. No one has yet resolved this problem. It has, moreover, been aggravated by the multi-national companies. Because of the sheer weight of resources put into an investment and bcause of the degree of automation achievable in modern manufacture, it is possible to site a new project in its most unlikely location and still produce goods at a cost advantage compared with older plants located in desirable spots and where vested interests exist. Recent investments in Eastern European countries and in the underdeveloped or developing regions are prime examples.

The answer to the problem may be global marketing, each nation behaving as a firm does, with a wide but comprehensive product range and a product mix subject to constant change.

As each company within the nation of companies must seek top management approval for development plans and the receipt of capital funds, it must first justify its aims on a global scale. Of course, this happens now through the functioning of the money market. But this system is purely nationalistic, when what is needed is a global attitude. In fact, one must apply marketing principles to the trading problems of nations rather than just of companies. The employment of trading blocs is a step in the right direction, although these partnerships tend to be defensive rather than offensive.

The major drawback of such a solution is in the selection of top management. Yet there is a possible remedy. As the twentieth century has shown a redistribution of influence as well as of income and wealth, it should not be impossible for top management to consist of industrialists, academics, trade unionists and professional administrators seconded from their respective posts for a period. As educational standards improve, the disparity in knowledge should decline, even if historical ideas and beliefs tend to consolidate.

The major marketing problem remains. It is in the need for common acceptance of popular products—the 'standardisation' of cultural beliefs, social habits, and moral and religious behaviour.

Mini-marketing

Some planners believe that by the year 2000 industry and commerce will be in the hands of a mere 200 companies, basing their conclusions partly on current trends and partly on a belief in the economies of scale. These business prophets appear to have ignored the invaluable part played by small companies in forcing large organisations to realise the economies of scale. Without pressure from the small firm, big business has little incentive to utilise its capacity for improving efficiency.

Competitive advantages

Also ignored are the competitive advantages the smaller unit
has over the bigger concern. A small firm with ambitions to
grow is often better placed to take advantage of marketing
opportunities than bigger companies. In an era of marketing
consciousness, where the customer plays such a significant
role in influencing commercial decision-making, it is the
business that discovers and satisfies a need which prospers.
The small company, because it has limited opportunities to
use mass media and because the number of its customers is
relatively low, is able to maintain a better line of communication with its markets at a personal level, through the salesman.
Thus, like the early worm, it is able to see opportunities
earlier. And because it does not have the cumbersome and
complicated, yet essential, decision-making process of the
larger organisation, it is able to initiate the means by which
market innovation takes place. Equally, because buyers recognise the need for standardisation in the product range of big
companies, they will take the special needs to the smaller firm.
The result may be the springboard for a new product idea or,
more simply, a 'special' for which the customer is prepared to
pay a premium price.

Often a small business with low overheads, specialist skills,
a limited product range, negligible marketing costs and established outlets with continual purchasing patterns (often found
in the engineering industry) will be able to produce parts,
subassemblies or components at a lower unit cost than a larger
company. Similarly, in some industries there are few sales
outlets and a limited demand for capital goods, which themselves are essential production units for large runs. The small
firm is often the only unit inclined to develop an economic
source of supply. Many buyers operating on behalf of international or multi-national companies favour the small firm to
supplement the limited range of a major supplier and so help
to ensure opportunity of choice as well as providing a lever to

force improvements in service by the often indifferent larger organisation. Apart from helping to minimise the consequences of the growing monopoly being created by large multi-product groups, the small firm enables the economic system to run smoothly.

The 'unreasonable man'

The small firm is the natural outlet for the energetic and determined individual who, perhaps having missed a satisfactory early education, decries the mediocrity of big business and its stifling effects on individual effort and enterprise. It is the ideal solution for enterprising and independent individuals whose vitality would be unsuited to the limitations of junior management in a large concern. It is this person, George Bernard Shaw's 'unreasonable man', whose entrepreneurial talent provides the initiative for devising and developing new products, techniques and services, a breeding ground for new industries.

The Report of the Committee of Enquiry on Small Firms (*The Bolton Report*) states: 'Apart from transport and communications, there are other aspects of marketing which have now come to enjoy substantial economies of scale. For example, improved techniques of distribution and the use of national media for advertising (themselves affected by technological change) are powerful factors working against the small firm. Indeed, we consider that lack of access (for the small firm) to economies in large scale marketing may be the most important single reason why the competitive strength of the larger firm has improved over the last fifty years.'

The small firms that are now forming marketing partnerships believe that these will enable them to compete on equal terms in the areas of marketing practice so far dominated by big firms. In this way the small firm retains its independence while improving its long-term competitiveness.

The major problems of mini-marketing are in finding and

exploiting minority needs. It has therefore a 'communication' problem to overcome. It must maintain contact with the few in the interests of the many.

The reader could not be blamed if, on reading this text, he is convinced that marketing is based on nothing more than common sense and the ability to communicate. He would be right. Unfortunately, common sense is rare, despite its name, and the ability to communicate equally rare. In combination their appearance represents a modern phenomenon. Finding personnel with the right talent is marketing's major continuing problem.

3 Marketing Research

The prime responsibility of the manager is decision-making.
A decision is a conclusion or a formal judgment precipitating
action. It is a process of evaluation and comparison. In order
to evaluate and compare it is necessary to have information.
Without information the basis for decisions is guesswork.
Occasionally, due to the law of averages, such intuitive efforts
succeed. Frequently, management actions are based on
experience alone and some measure of success may be achieved
for the same reason as intuitive actions.

Most managers will be aware of examples of successful ventures based on such meagre reasoning. With few exceptions,
such successes will have resulted despite the lack of information, not because the information was unnecessary. Risk in
business is endemic, but it should never be a gamble. In *The
Verger* Somerset Maugham brought elementary market
research graphically into perspective. The main character
decided to open a tobacconist's shop after walking a considerable distance to make a purchase. As he explained, he knew
from personal observation that the local demand was high. That
decision was based on information, obtained at negligible
expense; but even today projects costing many thousands of
pounds are initiated without adequate consideration of supply
and demand.

Marketing research is a process of investigation into the
workings of the distributive systems. Henry Ford, as has
already been mentioned, found through marketing research
the price at which cars would sell by the million and then

developed his mass production techniques accordingly (see his autobiography, *My Life and Work*). He was equating supply with demand.

Today, with the average size of company increasing, decisions have become even more critical. While a bad decision involving £5000 by a small firm may have more disastrous consequences than an equally bad decision involving £1 million by a large firm, the bigger investment decision may take two years to implement and a further three years before the outlay is recovered from profits. A time span of five years following a wrong decision could mean lost opportunities, frustrated management and an overall decline in company prosperity, far in excess of the project costs.

Judged against the changes in the past five years—in product innovation, channels of distribution, price levels and market needs—decisions made today require knowledge of future environment, events and human behaviour. Research into these influencing factors is essential.

It is almost 2500 years since Confucius said: 'Study the past if you would divine the future.' At that time, communications, transport facilities and human knowledge were decidedly poor. Production was confined to single items, so remedial decisions were easily made and quickly implemented. In the twentieth century this is not so. Divining the future must be more sophisticated. Industry and commerce is a mass of interdependent parts, cohesively manipulated by governments, with its appetite both nourished and deprived by world trade and by technological progress. Thus the past must be analysed, trends established and predictions made of innumerable influencing factors. Marketing research will not determine the future, but it can be used to illuminate the scene, to eliminate the unlikely and to spotlight the probable. It can help to reduce business risk.

Investigating investment

Research need not be costly. It should cost neither less than is justified nor more than is necessary in relation to the size or scale of investment. For example, when buying a new hat it is usually sufficient to visit the various stockists, compare styles and prices, and, if satisfied, make a purchase. When purchasing a house, it is normal for a more thorough investigation to be made. A survey of the property and its amenities is commissioned, and solicitors investigate legal title and any local planning developments. The prospective buyer, with the help of an estate agent, looks at local amenities, schools and recreational facilities. The building society will carry out its own independent inquiries. So the effort is equated according to the amount of expenditure. In each instance the extent of investigation is sufficient to meet the needs of the purchaser.

Many business decisions are made that could have been supported, or perhaps invalidated, by obtaining published information. Apart from internal records, most executives should be conversant with such official publications as *The Annual Abstract of Statistics*, the monthly *Digest of Statistics*, *The Blue Book of Income and Expenditure*, the *Department of Employment Gazette* and the *Censuses of Distribution*. In addition to the wealth of Government publications, such bodies as trade associations, banks, chambers of commerce, embassies, national and local newspapers, and the trade and technical press publish reports that can be invaluable to commerical concerns. A comprehensive list of sources and names and addresses is contained in the Institute of Marketing publication *Marketing Management: A World Register of Organisations*. This reference work provides data on organisations in 150 countries, and includes 1200 associations, institutions and para-governmental bodies. Many public libraries contain admirable works of reference and will often obtain information from other branches if it is not available locally.

One of the most comprehensive services provided for industry by the Department of Trade is the Statistics and Market Intelligence Library. Freely available for public use is a collection of trade and other economic statistics, trade directories and catalogues of manufacturers, which can be consulted either by personal visit, by telephone or by telex. Although the main purpose of the library is to provide a service in the field of foreign economic statistics, the library also holds complete sets of all the principal series of UK economic statistics.

An integral part of the British Institute of Management is the library at Management House. It contains the largest collection of management literature in Europe (over 40 000 items) and includes much unpublished material not generally available in this country. The library receives over 400 periodicals from all over the world; each is selectively scanned and indexed. Besides its lending services, the library has a valuable collection of reference material on management subjects. A wide range of specially prepared bibliographies helps those interested in particular subjects to keep abreast of current literature.

Apart from these libraries, there are many other sources of valuable information. The various National Economic Development Council departments prepare reports and publish their findings. Some trade associations make statistics available (see *Trade Associations and Professional Bodies of the UK* by Patricia Millard, published by Pergamon Press). *The Companies' Register* holds full financial information on all British companies, and many national newspapers maintain excellent information bureaux. *The Kompass Register* includes much company information and comprehensive details of products and services. There is a UK and an international edition of *Who Owns Whom*, compiled and published by Roskill & Co. *The Stock Exchange Year Book* is another valuable source of financial information.

Dun & Bradstreet publish a *British Middle Market Directory*, and *The Times* publishes annually a guide to the top 1000 companies in the UK. It is a visual comparative guide, by size and performance, to leading companies in the UK, the US, Europe, Japan and other countries. The top 1000 companies in the UK are ranked according to turnover and total sales. There is usually information on the fifty biggest mergers of the previous fiscal year. The Gower Economic Publications unit prepares similar studies on a number of European countries, as well as its 'off-the-shelf' market research into selected industries.

This list is not exhaustive and gives only an indication of the vast wealth of information readily available to industry. Few companies would fail to find some benefit in investigating sources relevant to their own operations.

Random sampling

Marketing research is frequently confused with market research. Marketing research is an activity that examines all the elements in marketing practice, including markets, products, distribution channels, pricing, consumer behaviour and opinions. Market research is but an element of marketing research, though easily the most widely known and practised. Opinion research is also a well-established operation. It has achieved recognition through public opinion polls. Predictions are made using sampling techniques, a fundamental part of marketing research. The concept of sampling (the law of probabilities) is that a number of items, if selected at random from a larger number of items, will tend to have much the same characteristics as the whole. Random selection means that every item of the whole must have a full and equal opportunity of being chosen.

In sampling a population of well over fifty million, complete 'random' selection is almost impossible to achieve. Opinion polls may be conducted in the streets and only persons accessible during that time are questioned. Where contact is made in the home, bias is possible as absentees are excluded and some people will not be willing to be interviewed; many others live in inaccessible places. Movement in population may be as high as 10% and so complete up-to-date lists will not be available.

In addition, whenever a mass selection of the population is sampled, there will be a certain error in the results, irrespective of whether the aim is to discover opinions of a political or commercial nature. Sometimes error can be introduced by smoothing or averaging. Since the adoption of a new code of practice for opinion pools, the five main companies in the field have been obliged to make available details of their methods of operation and the composition of their samples. The possibility of scrutiny should ensure that minimum acceptable standards will prevail. Nonetheless, such research activities are invaluable for policy or strategic decision-making. A 100% sample is almost impossible and would be unrealistic anyway; for example, only 70% or 80% of the population trouble to vote. Certainly in common research the limitations of sampling errors are more acceptable. Marketing executives are likely to understand the principles and will use the findings to exercise judgment and take action. They are another aid to decision-making but should not be allowed to rule the decisions.

It is now comparatively rare for completely random samples to be prepared—quota sampling is more often used. This is a technique whereby a controlled sample is selected which is known to represent the characteristics of the whole. It is relatively simple to build up a sample based on occupational groups, geographical areas, age brackets and community size. Because the margin of error is measurable, it is possible to apply confidence factors to most survey results. The ratio of the sample to the whole is not significant. Whatever the number of items in the whole, a sample of between 200 and 3000 items would tend to reflect the characteristics of the whole. Certainly the greater the size of the sample, the greater the accuracy, but the additional accuracy rarely justifies the extra expense. After all, the sole purpose of marketing research is to improve profitability.

The researcher's role

The difference between consumer research and industrial research is in the techniques used. The number of potential customers in consumer goods usually outnumber those in the industrial field by multiples of thousands. Industrial outlets are sparsely spread and contact is often difficult and uneconomic. The industrialist may have a maximum of 300 outlets, of which perhaps twenty or thirty may consume the bulk of his output. He must therefore maintain contact with his customers, whatever channels of distribution he uses. If he uses distributors or agents he must ensure that the technical needs of his customers are satisfied. Because he must be in contact constantly and because the number of his potential outlets is limited, he is more easily able to obtain information. Similar market information could only come to the consumer-goods company through expensive field research. Usually the researcher in industry is expected to have related technical knowledge and relevant industrial background. In this way he will be able to win the confidence of both customer and employer, ensuring satisfactory communication between the two.

Field research may be conducted by postal questionnaire, telephone interviews or personal visits. Postal questionnaires have the advantage of economy, although the response rate may be low. Any conclusions drawn will have a built-in bias since people who tend to be mobile will not be represented, nor will those who habitually ignore research efforts. Telephone interviewing has the major advantage of time as contact is immediate and interviewers are able to explain the purpose of the survey. Answers may be recorded without the respondent being disturbed about the possible repercussions of his observations. The response rate is usually higher than with postal questionnaires. Bias is introduced because only those respondents available by telephone can be contacted. It is also impossible for the interviewer to obtain information by observation. Personal interviewing is usually the most reliable means of obtaining information, but it is expensive. To obtain the best results and to minimise the disadvantages of each technique, it is usual for a survey to use all three means of contact, structuring the sample according to predetermined criteria.

Questionnaire design

Most research studies are undertaken using a questionnaire. Often it is designed using principles established by a working study committee of the Market Research Society. As the research is carried out to determine a given business situation and the reasons for the currency of that situation, question-naires are designed to help to assess the habits and prejudices of the chosen group of people that constitute the market. Clearly, to be useful and valuable, the answers must come as a result of well-worded and presented questions. To get the right answers one must ask the right questions. So a specific set of objectives is essential.

Questionnaires are used to ensure that the many inter-viewers being employed in different parts of the country carry out their interviews in as near identical fashion as possible. They ask the same questions and use the same terms. By using a questionnaire it is possible to ensure that answers provided by respondents, whether at a personal inter-view or otherwise, are recorded in a predetermined fashion. This makes it easy for the forms, and the answers, to be coded for analysis, particularly where a computer is to be used.

However, questionnaires have to be carefully designed. A poorly designed questionnaire will throw all the research findings into doubt, so its design must follow fairly simple principles. Providing the research project with a clear aim based on predetermined objectives is the first step. This should then be followed by a number of rules:

1 The central theme of the enquiry must be clear.
2 The interviewees' memories must not be overtaxed.
3 Every question must be clear.
4 Psychological factors must be anticipated.
5 Leading questions must be avoided.
6 Questions should follow a logical sequence.
7 The language of the informant must be used.
8 Questions must not restrict the interviewee.
9 Misleading questions must be avoided.
10 Questionnaires should be short and simple.
11 Questions should be confined to the personal experience of respondents.
12 Control questions should be introduced.

Although these rules may appear straightforward they are nonetheless broken sufficiently often to warrant an explanation.

1 The central theme of the enquiry must be clear
Enquiries are usually directed at particular users of a product, service or machine, so users must be identified in the first instance. If usage of the item concerned is the central theme of the research, then answers from non-users are irrelevant.

2 The interviewees' memories must not be overtaxed
People do not like to admit that their memories have failed them, particularly if there is an inference, as in a questionnaire, that they should be able to recall an event or incident. To overtax the interviewees' memories will introduce answers of doubtful validity and value.

3 Every question must be clear
Good communication is difficult to achieve and without supporting explanation often impossible. Yet to produce reliable information, unambiguous questions must be asked. So all

questions need to be pre-tested. Studying the answers will indicate the clarity or otherwise of the questions concerned.

4   *Psychological factors must be anticipated*
Informants tend to offer what they consider to be the right answers rather than to express the exact truth. To a number of people an affirmative answer on usage of a deodorant could be taken as an admission of body odour. Similarly, the readership of quality newspapers is often overstated, as respondents give what are thought to be socially acceptable replies.

5   *Leading questions must be avoided*
People do not like to offend. In addition, experience has probably taught them that contrary answers invite exploration and their time is limited. So they seek from tone, manner, gesture or whatever some sign of the approved or right answer. Any question that suggests a particular reply will most often get it. The results will therefore be invalid.

6   *Questions should follow a logical sequence*
As people are taught from the beginning of their education to think in sequence, it is advisable to follow that pattern. Most respondents will follow the sense of questions and so answers will come from reasoning rather than intuitively.

7   *The language of the informant must be used*
Many people use a language common to particular groups but foreign to outsiders. Accountants, engineers and apparently, marketing men use their own special language—a practice to be avoided when questioning people who may not be aware of the special meanings that certain words have acquired.

8   *Questions must not restrict the interviewee*
The interviewee should be given a choice of possible answers to a question sufficient to produce the response most appro-

priate to his or her particular experience. To give straight alternatives makes choice difficult and sometimes onerous to people with knowledge lying somewhere between the extremes.

9 Misleading questions must be avoided

Misleading questions tend to arise whenever salesmen are used for research projects. It is not that they intend to mislead but that their enthusiasm is frustrated if the respondent ponders too long. So the salesman will try to help him out by asking a supplementary question which is often misleading.

10 Questionnaires should be short and simple

There is a common belief among market researchers that every question over twenty in number in a research study will cost 5% in lost response. Trying to extract too much information from one survey may therefore destroy the representative nature of the sample frame.

11 Questions should be confined to the personal experience of respondents

No matter how qualified they may feel to answer questions on behalf of their boss or spouse, third-party evidence is often totally misleading. It is difficult enough for the individual to know why a particular action is taken, let alone why someone else might do so. It is better for the researcher not to take the chance.

12 Control questions should be introduced

It is advisable to include a question that relates to an earlier one so as to establish a reliability factor in the informant. Sometimes researchers will also include a sample reliability question in order to test the validity of the selected sample.

These are sound principles of questionnaire design. Even when followed exactly it is still necessary to check whether the design is satisfactory. This is best done with a pilot test using about 10% of the proposed sample frame. A questionnaire should always be tested.

Depth interviewing

This is a technique used to discover the extent of a person's knowledge in a particular field and the underlying reasons behind his or her actions. It is not normally conducted using a questionnaire and tends to be much less formal, with the investigator guiding the conversation along from a list of points. The role of the interviewer is more like that of a prompter, even perhaps a sympathetic listener, rather than an examiner. The informant is allowed to develop his own lines of thought provided that they remain relevant to the enquiry. The major task of the interrogator is to help the respondent relax so that he is able to bring latent thoughts and motives to the surface.

It is generally believed that depth interviewing makes it easier to secure evidence of a person's attitude of mind or even his emotional feelings than is possible within the confines of a formal questionnaire. Its greatest use perhaps is in the absence of other information, when material obtained using depth interviews may then be used in the construction of a questionnaire appropriate for a more formal study. Its enthusiasts claim that it is the only reliable means of testing advertising and sales promotional material. Presumably qualitative techniques of research into areas where publicity strategies are unavoidably qualitative has some logic. In practice there are good reasons why the technique has limited acceptance. Few people are capable of explaining their opinions and even fewer their emotions. So this makes the technique as vulnerable as formal questionnaires. Psychologists question the basis of the system believing that the use of introspection provides a stimulus, for by the introduction of one thought we create another which was not present in connection with the held opinions. So a response would tend to be too educated to reflect the original view. In any case, usable conclusions cannot be expressed qualitatively and this makes it difficult to get some measure of the collective results.

It seems unlikely that depth interviewing will produce the results expected of it until some better means of interview recording is used, a realistic sample of consumers is tested so that standards of behaviour may be prepared and tabulated, and until psychologists are prepared to conduct the interviews rather than leaving them to unqualified researchers.

Motivational research

However, depth interviewing has been awarded some distinction, particularly in the field of motivational research. Credited to this form of qualitative research are successes in redirecting the advertising theme for cake-mixes to 'add an egg', so that the housewife may feel she is actually baking the cake, and in restructuring the campaign for instant coffee after it was realised that housewives associated the product with laziness.

The technique has, however, lost much of its momentum due principally to overemphasis. Its supporters tended to seek association between products and ideas that were less than credible. Links between tomato soup and amniotic fluid were suggested, as were extra-sharp razor-blades and castration complexes. Irrespective of the truth of these bizarre claims, they were ridiculed and confidence in the method was affected.

Classifying the consumer

An analysis of research information would almost certainly prove fruitless if the total population were treated as one whole group. Clearly within one nation there are many subgroups that have characteristics common to the group and yet foreign to the remainder. The total population is therefore often divided into identifiable groups. These groups are normally:

1 Socio-economic groupings
2 Sex
3 Age
4 Occupation
5 Area or region

Apart from socio-economic groupings, these classifications need no further explanation. Socio-economic groupings leave much to be desired and are not now in general use. But they are still the subject of frequent reference in conversation, particularly in the advertising world. A means of categorising the nation is a vital aid to the mass media, particularly from a readership angle. However, there is no alternative to the socio-economic group analysis. In this method the total population is subdivided by a combination of social position and earning power. For example, a member of the professional services, such as a barrister or a priest, will be included in the most affluent group irrespective of their earnings, qualifying because of their social position. Newspapers often provide information on their readership by socio-economic groups. It enables them to help advertisers to decide the most appropriate medium for their campaigns. Clearly the more expensive commodities of life will be bought by the well-to-do and an advertisement aimed at them will appear in a publication popular in that group.

Consumer panels

Since the major benefit of market research is the discovery of trends and changes in purchasing habits, it is necessary to carry out research on a continuous basis rather than from time to time in an ad hoc fashion. These continuous research studies enable advertisers to observe consumers' changing tastes, their buying habits, opinions and brand preferences. So declines in sales can be anticipated and remedial action taken. The sample used in these studies is semi-permanent and questioning is undertaken at regular intervals. These samples are known as panels and may be either groups of dealers or groups of consumers. The dealer panels provide a valuable insight into the attitudes of the trade towards a company and its products. The consumer panels, however, provide the most critical information and have many positive benefits:

1 Trends can be established.
2 Past behaviour is already recorded.
3 The cost of the panel may be shared.
4 The nature of the research allows intimate questioning.
5 It is not necessary to rely on consumers' memories.
6 Unreliable informants are soon spotted and dropped.
7 Changes in tastes precipitate action in the market place.

A number of disadvantages, however, are apparent. Maintaining the panel and its members' co-operation is a continuing problem, while having to submit to the discipline of a regular record of behaviour tends to inhibit natural behaviour. The administration of the panel can be expensive, requiring constant checking of detail and supervision of certain members' tendency to understate their purchases of cheaper brands.

Retailer audits

The Nielsen Continuous Index type of research was introduced into the UK just before the outbreak of the last war in 1939. It consists of a team of auditors who make regular visits to a selected panel of retailers representative of the retail trade and count the actual stock and invoiced purchases for the period since the last count. Its major benefit in research terms is as a measure of the flow of goods to consumers. As such, it provides information on the rate at which goods are passing through the channels of distribution.

When a product goes out of fashion its sales will decline at the point of purchase, but the trade may still order as before and there may be no indication of the forthcoming calamity.

And, of course, the trade will not appreciate being left with unsaleable goods.

Nielsen's provide a fairly comprehensive coverage in their reports, but the following categories are typical:

1 Sales to consumers by product and by brand.
2 Sales to retailers by product and by brand.
3 Current stocks by product and by brand.
4 Percentage of outlets handling the various brands.
5 Percentage of outlets with stock outs for various brands.
6 Retail and wholesale selling prices by product.
7 Volume of business handled direct and through wholesalers.
8 The extent of display and the sales scheme in operation at each outlet by various brands.

This service enables the subscriber to vet trends among his own and his competitors' brands, and to isolate problem areas by one or more of the main geographical regions or by one or more of the three sizes of shop shown. It means that every manufacturer knows the share he has and the changes in shares between himself and his competitors. This information is more than just useful. It can indicate how a company's growth in sales compares with growth in the total market and, if there is a decline, whether it is confined to the company or is industry-wide. The indices provided by the Nielsen organisation cover food, drugs, tobacco, pharmaceuticals and confectionery. The firm also produces an index on liquor from Scotland.

Many of the benefits of the system approximate to those listed under consumer panels. In addition, it provides information on distribution of a product, effect of price changes, promotions and advertising. But it tends to be expensive, is not truly representative because some multiples will not co-operate, and figures are calculated in complicated forms, not always inspiring confidence in the heart of the subscriber. By definition its findings are quantitative, so although it indicates what, where and when it does not provide information on the vital areas of why and how.

Test marketing

The value of test marketing is hotly disputed. Its supporters believe it is the only means by which a company is able to overcome teething problems before going national and before irreparable damage takes place. Others say that it warns competition, and that regions do not truly reflect national characteristics and therefore tests are invalid.

Clearly there is sense in each argument. The organisers of test marketing operations must, therefore, recognise the limitationsof the technique and use it to their advantage. The best value can be obtained in:

1 Formulating a national introductory plan.
2 Deciding the best media available for the product.
3 Choosing the most effective level of advertising.
4 Selecting the appropriate price level for maximising profit.

The golden rule is to carry out tests in at least two areas and to investigate every disparity that arises. In each area the tests should be considered as separate activities.

A test will fail if the new product is given special support while in the introductory stage. Even the presence of the marketing manager during the launch constitutes additional support. The most usual support of this sort discovered is:

1 Presence of 'authority' at local branch.
2 Heavier advertising support than is possible nationally.
3 Giving the product a 'fair chance' by using the territory or the best salesman as a testing ground.

To be considered successful a product must stand the test of time—the time to include repeat purchases. Where national performance lags behind the hopes generated for it by the test market, it is either because of the over-emphasis already described or because the decision to launch nationally has been taken before the test promotion has matured.

Conditions for concluding that the new product satisfies the test marketing objectives are:

1   That initial response has been generated according to plan.
2   That repeat purchases are now being made.
3   That the consumer is making repeat purchases in normal conditions and not in the tidal wave of launch.
4   That the longer term (six months to a year) shows a steady acceptance of the product and continuing growth.
5   When inconsistencies in plan appear and are resolved through contingencies.

It should be understood that test marketing is not a product test. The product will have been tested and tried prior to the pilot venture. The test marketing project is to test the *marketing* of the product—to confirm the adequacies of the planned marketing mix. However, it can often be used as a final test of *acceptance* for the product, although in a sense this is a check on the company's ability to market the product and not a trial of the product's worthiness.

Measuring advertising effectiveness

Some activities of marketing can be quantified in some way. One exception is advertising. To some companies the advertising appropriation is the biggest single item of expenditure in the marketing budget. Yet no one has been able to measure the extent to which advertising increases sales. Because advertising is usually so closely tied to exploiting the concept of marketing, it is not always possible to isolate it from other marketing activities. There are some exceptions. Mail order houses are able to measure trends in effectiveness because advertising and sales promotion is almost all of their promotional effort. We do, however, know that advertising works. We may not know the exact level at which expenditure may be justified, but we do know that the expenditure can be effective.

How, then, can one deal with advertising expenditure objectively? A change in attitude and approach is necessary. The businessman must move away from attempting to measure the effectiveness of the advertising *function*, which is to *inform* and to *persuade*. As the basis of marketing research is one of evaluation and comparison, a standard of performance must be established. Without a predetermined standard, objective measurement is not possible. The critical issue is: 'what do we want our advertising to achieve?' If it is necessary, for example, to increase public awareness of the product, then this will be the advertising function. Research may reveal that only 10% of prospective customers know of a product. Research may show that the other 90% can be contacted through a given medium. The campaign, the appropriation and advertising objectives thus become clear. Measurement of effectiveness is made by further research to reveal the increased awareness of the product by the market.

Marketing research is a valuable tool of management. The growing complexity of business operations makes its greater and more widespread use essential. It is a vital part of profit planning and needs to be used to obtain information essential for decision-making.

4 Product Planning and Pricing

To understand marketing philosophy it is first necessary to consider the nature of product satisfaction. For what is a product? Consider jewellery. Does the average person buy an expensive ring because of the utility of this purchase or is there some underlying purpose? Why should a person 'trade-up' from a Mini to a Rover? For what reason do people buy cosmetics? A jewel may have no real value, while a Mini will take a person from one place to another quite satisfactorily, and cosmetics are but waxes and greases of comparatively little value in the untreated state. Clearly the purchaser is buying some satisfaction which is identified with the product rather than with the primary purpose for which the product has been made available.

A ring denotes genuine affection. It has connotations with love and marriage. Between young people it is, perhaps, the ultimate material gift. It signifies the value placed on the relationship and the durability of the union. It suggests promise for the future—a promise of happiness even—together. Similarly, buying a more expensive car is a symbol of progress. It is a gesture of defiance to friends, or a quest for approval from relations, and an expression of self-assurance before the opposite sex, for the motor car has been described as the ultimate sex-symbol. And cosmetics are not required because of their ability to create beauty but because of their confidence-building capacity. It follows that the purchasers of these products are, in turn, buying a symbol of love, social approval and self-confidence. So the product concerned, for each of them, does no more than provide the means by which a need is fulfilled. Thus a product may be defined as a 'conveyor-belt of satisfactions', not so very different in meaning from the classical economists' 'bundle of utilities'. The important factors that arise from these conclusions are that totally different products may be competing against each other for the same purpose, while marketing communications aimed at *product utility* will have little or no effect on consumer motivation.

In today's society output at one factory may have little to distinguish it from the output of a competitive factory. In the market place, however, the same products may have totally different sales performances. Because the marketing of one product may have provided so much 'added value' it becomes a much better proposition to the buyer. These added values may take the form of packaging, financing, services, distribution, advertising, customer advice, delivery, storage or whatever it is that makes it convenient to the consumer. So the product must provide satisfaction to innate desires as well as function mechanically, and it must be marketed in a way that enables the buyer to achieve the greatest possible satisfaction at the lowest possible expenditure of time, effort and money. Products of the future need to conform to this specification in order to succeed. But success is relative, for some successes are confined to a few short months, while others may endure for many generations.

The product life cycle

Fashion goods may enjoy buoyant sales for one season only, while basic industries such as coal or iron extraction have experienced growth in sales performance for centuries. Yet in each case it is necessary for the marketing executive to recognise the evolutionary nature of each product's life span. The marketing executive associated with fashion goods knows that the market situation is volatile and that a constant stream of new designs is essential. For without new creations the fashion industry would cease to be in *fashion* and would have to resort to *clothing*. Fashion is a more attractive market because the level of expenditure necessary to accommodate a person's need for style is greater than their level of expenditure on clothes for warmth, modesty and convention.

In the extractive industries the position is quite different, for coal and iron ore remain much the same, despite frequent attempts to improve the product. But the marketing manager has an equally arduous task, because although he has little chance to adapt the product he has almost complete versatility in the market segments open to him.

In each case the product life cycle has similar characteristics but the time span is different. Moreover, that time span puts different pressures on the marketing team and the company's corporate strategy evolves accordingly.

Each product goes through four stages:

1 Introduction
2 Growth
3 Maturity
4 Decline

The duration of each stage varies considerably. Clearly the use of the product life cycle concept is only of real value if each stage in its curve is predictable, because once achieved it would suggest a means by which demand could be varied according to the level of marketing expenditure, and so it would bring a revolution in marketing practice with consequences as memorable as those that followed the industrial revolution. Mathematics has been used to differentiate the curve of the product life cycle, but the method, unfortunately, requires at least one constant. And what in marketing remains unchanged?

The product manager

Despite the now universal acceptance of marketing as a business function, few companies have carried out any real reorganisation of their companies beyond changing the name of the sales manager and expecting him to perform the marketing miracle. This approach is so common that one suspects a latent rejection of marketing principles and no more than a token acceptance of the activities of marketing. However, those companies recognising the difficulties in changing established attitudes and ideas have reorganised their management structure to provide a co-ordinator of the established functional management tasks. As it is not possible for authority to be taken from functional heads without also relieving them of their responsibilities, product managers, or brand managers as they might otherwise be called, are expected to extract improved performance from each department by providing an information system. The information system is expected to increase the productivity of each department by improving decision-making. The product manager achieves his mission by developing the marketing plan, in co-operation with functional heads, and then co-ordinates the agreed actions. The final plan will be monitored by him.

So the product manager has no authority. But he does have considerable responsibility. For he is held to be a mini-managing director for a brand or a product group. He achieves his objectives by investigating, interpreting and recommending action over changes in the pattern of demand. He achieves this requirement in four stages:

1 Understanding the market
2 Investigating the competition
3 Attracting new product ideas
4 Developing the product image

These activities are the essence of the product manager's job. They are fundamental to product planning in a marketing-orientated company. The evolution of each step provides the qualitative side to the more quantitative aims of marketing research.

1 Understanding the market

The share of a specific market obtained by any particular company is subject to constant change. It may be caused by pricing strategy, by product innovation or by new product development. The forces of competition are among the most difficult to predict of all the variables facing the businessman. It is not always easy to decide which competitors are most likely to be active at any foreseeable time in the future. It is necessary, however, to prophesy which products from the competitors' ranges, and which of their areas, are likely to be given special promotion.

Frequently the decisions made within a company will be the result of internal political manoeuvring and strength of personality. Even these influences are subject to rapid change. Often a particularly aggressive promotional campaign by one company will expand the total market and others will benefit. For example, when a manufacturer of soups with a 50% level of distribution among retail outlets advertises on television, he may stimulate interest and invite consumers to try the product for the first time. Those enquiring at their local store and finding the goods unavailable may be diverted to an alternative. The same principle can apply in industrial markets. A salesman may interest a prospect in a money-saving piece of equipment. The prospect may then contact his regular supplier of industrial equipment, with whom he has a good relationship, hoping he has a similar product. This stimulus may even produce a demand for suitable alternatives. The businessman who has been interested by a computer salesman may begin investigations in data processing in general and, for example, decide on a real-time computer service. Hence there would be little change or upheaval, so frequently associated with the installation of a computer, in his present system of working.

So, in evaluating competitive influences, it is necessary first to evaluate the impact general economic influences may have

upon the industry as a whole. Frequently government legislation can cause a shift in the pattern of demand; for example,
discontinuing tax concessions for entertainment expenditure
caused a temporary setback to many catering establishments.
Money not spent on entertainment was then channelled
into other areas. Often the growth of a totally unrelated
industry affects the performance of others. The rapid growth
of the petro-chemical industry and the increasing use and
storage of combustible materials have probably stimulated the
demand for fire detection, alarm and defence systems, particularly sprinklers. Fortunately, many of these external
influences are predictable. Certainly there will be any amount
of published comment and opinion which will often indicate
likely possibilities. Usually trade associations and professional
institutions make representations on proposed government
legislation, while recognised authoritative writers suggest the
possible consequences of economic developments. For the
vigilant, external influences to a particular industry can be
noted and the consequences assessed. Constant review of the
trade and technical press, the business news and city sections
of national newspapers helps the enlightened businessman to
ensure that he is aware of future events and possibilities.

Monitoring external influences becomes more complex
during periods of economic instability. It may still be necessary
to evaluate the extent to which competitors are likely to affect
business prospects during any given period of time. Often
competitors for available purchasing power become confused
with competitors for substitute products. Sausage is easily
recognisable as a substitute for meat but during hard times
bread and potatoes—competitors for purchasing power—
become substitute products as well: *less* meat, *more* potatoes.
A competitor evaluation is an integral part of the marketing
plan, for, whether active or passive, all competitors' actions
influencet he performance of other companies within the industry. If a company is experiencing a bad spell or liquidation,
its death throes could cause an upheaval in the market. It may

choose price cutting as the easiest solution to its problems; other companies anxious to maintain their market share may match the lower prices, and the general level of profitability will drop.

Apart from price cutting, the events that frequently cause a change in the usual market pattern are:

(a)   Product innovation
(b)   Product substitution
(c)   Government legislation
(d)   Product obsolescence
(e)   Changes in taste or fashion
(f)   Seasonal factors
(g)   Import quotas
(h)   Trade recessions
(i)   Strikes and industrial disputes
(j)   Changes in distribution margins

2   Investigating the competition

To decide just what course of action competitors are likely to take in any given circumstances will frequently be perplexing. Often information is obtainable with little effort. Customers often report a planned launch of a new product by a competitor. To obtain information on the likely sales strategy may be possible by watching the classified advertisement columns of the trade and technical press or of the national newspapers. It is surprising how much useful information companies reveal in their search for staff. Even the use of box numbers or selection consultants does not always conceal a company's identity, particularly to the discerning businessman who has anticipated some such action on the part of a competitor.

When no supporting information is available, the best action to take is to consider what information would be needed to make a decision and what choice would be made if the investigator had to decide. This rule of thumb usually produces a number of logical paths that may be taken, each of which may produce similar results. So, from an infinite number of variables, the choice has been reduced to just a few. Flexible counterplans may now be prepared which can be actioned as soon as further information becomes available. In a number of instances it is known that competing marketing executives exchange information relevant to their development.

The 1967 Companies Act has made it possible for an investigator to obtain substantial financial information on competitors. The exempt private company no longer exists; such companies are compelled by law to file a profit and loss account and a balance sheet with their annual returns. Information about companies is readily available from Companies' House in London. However, a breakdown between product groups is not provided. So companies competing against others with diverse product ranges and selling to different markets will have some difficulty in assessing the sales turnover achieved by those companies in the field being investigated.

In making a comparison between competitive firms it is logical to assume that, whatever the extent of market penetration achieved by firms, the success or otherwise of their achievements is attributable to some activity on their part. One firm may have a strong sales force, another may spend considerable sums on advertising. Whatever the cause, it should be isolated. In drawing up a league table of competitors the businessman should develop a means of weighing up these activities. They will vary according to industry, but they will normally include:

(a) Pricing strategy
(b) Sales-force strength
(c) Advertising effectiveness
(d) Product advantages
(e) Past reputation
(f) Distribution facilities

By progressively developing a league table it should soon be possible to establish measurement of the comparative effectiveness of the tools of marketing activity. Combining these factors with changing market shares should indicate the division into which future promotional budgets should be prepared.

3 Attracting new product ideas

In this competitive environment unique product advantages are short-lived since others will copy successful innovation or make further improvements. If the growth rate of net profit is to be maintained a company must initiate a new product-development programme, particularly when confronted with escalating marketing costs for established products. Even those companies that have already established new product departments need to improve still more the ratio of successful to unsuccessful products. There are three different methods by which new product ideas can be brought to the attention of a company.

Members of the sales force constantly report on ideas given to them by customers and prospects, while the company's own production and research people and executives will be constantly suggesting new product possibilities. Outside the company, suggestions may come from independent inventors, distributors, suppliers, advertising agents, the trade press and even competitors.

The ideas emanating from external sources are usually spontaneous thoughts which may or may not have validity in terms of markets sales potential. Often external ideas are the major source of suggestions and the system frequently brings a high failure rate.

Less frequently, but more effectively, a company may make a conscious effort to study systematically the markets it satisfies in an endeavour to establish new needs, or old needs that have never been properly satisfied. This is known as *gap analysis*, and where opportunities are uncovered a suitable product can be introduced and the known benefits heavily promoted.

Resources. Logically, this approach could be adopted by all companies; it makes use of present market knowledge, is within the company's own business activity and in an area of operation where marketing skills have already been tried.

In evaluating such needs a company may find that a small company has been specialising in the satisfaction of a current need but does not have the resources, or perhaps the inclination, to develop the market to its full potential.

The acquisition of such a company may prove a sound investment, as established business can be obtained with much of the development costs written off, together with personnel having experience and knowledge of uses to which the products may be put and of the applications that have already been established.

The new product-development team must be assured of a constant stream of ideas from the sources already suggested or as a result of regular brain-storming sessions. Ideally, new product ideas will come from the marketing research team, although occasionally suggestions from research and development may need to be tested in terms of market acceptability before any attempt is made to commercialise them.

Before finalising a development programme it is always advisable to carry out a preliminary appraisal of the commerical feasibility of each project. This study should include desk research in an effort to compile as much associated information as possible relevant to the product's development, production, promotion and acceptance.

At the same time the researchers will have consultations with all known qualified opinion from within the company and, as far as possible, outside the company. Attempts will have to be made to test the likely market sales potential and the sales volume that may be achieved at each time-stage after the product's launch. The expected product design and specification is identified and recorded, while all packaging considerations are listed.

A network of timing for launch and related promotional activities is prepared with pricing proposals clearly shown, along with the anticipated costs of capital development. Additional labour requirements are specified and the promotional and other marketing costs budgeted.

Sales volume. If after this thorough screening process the new product idea is considered satisfactory, a full development programme may be formulated with confidence. In making this feasibility study the company is clearly basing its future upon perceived and measured market needs.

At the outset it should be established whether the new product is intended to bring a higher sales volume in order to take up surplus manufacturing capacity or whether it is intended to provide more profitable sales volume by replacing, ultimately, products that may have a declining rate of profitability.

Any such policy statement should specify whether an expansion, or more successful operation, is intended in established markets or whether an entry is planned into new markets which may offer better profit potential.

When entering a new market, executives tend to recognise the limitations of their market knowledge and even consider deeply the possible inadequacies of their marketing effort in promoting the new product successfully. What many executives do not recognise is that with a constantly changing market situation the same principle will often apply to the market with which they do have knowledge and experience.

Test marketing a product in a chosen area which statistically and by observation tends to represent the characteristics of the total market is used effectively by a number of companies. One of the most difficult parts of test marketing is, in fact, the selection of the trial area. It is never easy to choose the necessary level of expenditure for one isolated area that would equate with a national launch. An area is usually chosen because it contains sufficient purchasers to provide a realistic sample and yet is small enough to be covered economically with suitable control.

Purchasers. To market an industrial product, which may vary in sales volume according to the type of purchaser, it is necessary to establish the different types of purchasers in the test area and how they compare with the national concentration. The area must be one that has advertising media and a local sales force which are typical of the whole country.

If the new product is intended to fill a gap in an existing range, the competitive strength of the launching company must be compared with that of others in the area and related to national market shares before any worthwhile conclusions can be drawn.

4 Developing the product image

Even selling internationally, the marketing man must strive to create a product image. People tend to associate countries with certain goods and services. For example, Switzerland will be associated with watches, banking services and winter sports; Holland with diamonds, tulips and cheese. Most industrially advanced countries can be associated in this way with particular products. In many instances the product and the country of origin have become linked together—for example, Scotch whisky, Swiss watches, Danish bacon. In overcoming such established images the marketing man may have to spend considerable time in educating his future market.

Many goods once considered luxuries are now accepted as necessities of life. Since the day when Henry Ford set out to find the price at which cars would sell by the million, manufacturers have increasingly tried to price their products to appeal to mass markets. Inevitably this has meant standardisation. Popular prices can be achieved only through mass production, and mass production must mean the elimination of some choice. The larger firms usually concentrate on satisfying the mass markets, with consumers clamouring for goods that they can now afford. Without large-scale production and the prices that result, most consumers would be unable to buy these goods. The limitation of choice is the additional price to be paid for such products. The smaller firm tends to concentrate on the provision of more specialised goods which the minority will always demand and for which they are prepared to pay a higher price.

In developing mass markets the larger manufacturer must devote his total resources to promoting popular products through emphasis on particular qualities that the product possesses. Sometimes these benefits may be apparent, but often they are contrived in order to provide a company with a unique selling proposition. In creating a unique image companies frequently achieve a monopoly. This monopoly is a direct result of brand loyalty and not because of limitation on sources of supply. Often the manufacturer's name becomes almost a generic term for the product itself. Few people would need an explanation of the products associated with Hoover, Sellotape, Biro, Vaseline or Aspro. Occasionally, such manufacturers are able to charge a premium on the price of their products.

It is on perceptive interpretation of potential market needs that progressive companies prosper. It is by finding a need, assessing the potential and, where substantial, taking the necessary action to satisfy the need that true market orientation becomes apparent. It is not enough for companies to provide production capacity. The market for a product has to be prepared, particularly where the need is still latent.

Pricing

It seems common among firms for pricing decisions to be made on the information supplied by accountants based on analysis of costs. Although most trained managers would recognise this as inadequate, few are able to suggest the means by which a better alternative, the market price, is implemented. For although market pricing may be the accepted technique, the experts are unable to produce the evidence upon which such a price may be calculated.

The market price itself escapes definitive expression. After all, many firms are unable to define their market, let alone the prices its members would be prepared to pay. Most suppliers are unable to put a 'cost' on the market value of a product acceptable to its purchasers. This is hardly surprising when one considers the disputed alternatives on return-on-investment appraisal. Probably the purchasing company itself does not know the value of a capital equipment purchase. If it does, it is unlikely to be adamant about the accuracy of its calculations, and it is certainly equally unlikely to reveal its costings to a supplier. A wholly-owned subsidiary may be prepared to release such calculations; in fact, it probably had to, to gain top management approval for the investment, so the figures would be available. But, judging by the controversy over transfer pricing, it seems unlikely that associated companies are in a position to help each other over the calculation of a market price. Moreover, the market price itself may not be at one level; it may even be possible at a number of platforms. The total potential demand for a product may therefore range between broad parameters. People buying a Rolls Royce motor car may be quite indifferent to the price. In fact, if the price were doubled, it is conceivable that the demand would grow because the value of certain goods is judged by its price alone. Consider this example. An importer sold a small consignment of Russian salmon to a retailer. Some weeks later the importer checked and found that the retailer had sold one tin. On hearing that the one sale had been 'for the cat' and that it had been sold at 1/6 compared with the price of 3/6 for the regular English tin, he, the supplier, suggested a selling price of 7/-. As a result, the consignment was sold in three days. It had sold as a luxury product comparable even to caviar.

Greengrocers and fruiterers are well aware of the peculiarities of the consumer. Put a case of apples up for sale at 7p per lb and sales will be moderate. Put the same apples in three displays selling at 6p, 7p and 8p and sales will be healthy, particularly at 7p. When the display at 7p is emptying it is replenished from the other two. People like to choose something to suit their own individual ideas, and usually it will not be too dear and certainly not the cheapest. A certain butcher has a thriving business because he knows how to treat his customers. One late arrival seeing a solitary chicken in the display cabinet asked if he had anything larger. Taking the last bird with him into the walk-in ice-room he said he had been closing up for the day and that there were others in the store. Returning in seconds with the same bird and a higher price tag he enquired if this one would do. The customer was delighted. He charged her the original lower price and everyone was happy.

Incremental pricing theory
Pricing has such problems. A story told by Roy Jenkins of Quantum Sciences Ltd is an example of profitable pricing 'under cost'.

A barrow boy sets out from home in the morning with £25 in his pocket and buys fifty shirts. He sells his first one at 9.00 a.m. for £1 and thinks 'that's a start, we'll see how they go at that'. By midday he has sold twenty-five at £1 each. After lunch he sells another at £1 and thinks 'that's a £1 profit'. At 4.00 p.m. he has ten left and sells them at 40p each—still at a profit. The last one he sells to the man at the next barrow for 5p—still at a profit. Accountants will shudder.

These concepts of profit are very easy to apply in such circumstances, but they become so much more complex in larger organisations and where many people and activities are involved. Yet the basic principles still apply. Many an organisation will sell the bulk of its output below its computed 'cost', because the cost includes a full recovery of overheads at a particular level of operation. Change that level and the whole cost structure alters. But selling the bulk of its output below this cost enables the company to use production systems totally uneconomic at a smaller scale but highly cost-effective at the level at which the firm operates. The profitability achieved on the balance of its production overcompensates for the prices charged to the big buyers. The supplier is maximising his profits. This incremental costing system carries risks. But the profits it earns are the rewards it gets for risk bearing.

Pricing in the marketing mix

Because so many companies choose to use prices as their major strategy, pricing has been assured a position of isolation from the marketing mix. Moreover, because of this, it is essential to differentiate between pricing strategy and pricing tactics. This is not always easy because they are often interdependent. A company may decide to slot into a particular market at a specific price level and it develops a product accordingly. That is pricing strategy. It is the basis of Henry Ford's success with the Model T and is the underlying strategy behind the Japanese growth. The organisation aims at the most vulnerable price level ripe for exploitation. Once the price level has been established, necessary variations in the price structure day to day are tactical.

Price is, however, but one element in the marketing mix. Often it is no more that a substitute for other marketing activities. A low pricing level may be a substitute for a strong sales force, or it may be an alternative to promotional activity. Although it has been shown that sound marketing reduces prices, it is often pressure from the least efficient concerns, those that cut prices to survive in the face of powerful marketing, that brings the industry price level within the pockets of the less well-to-do.

Pricing techniques

Most companies are engaged in a marketing battle which is attempting to break the incidence of demand curves or at least to bend them in their own favour. The usual techniques for this objective are:

1 Penetration price
2 Skimming price

3   Competitive price
4   Diversionary price
5   Dumping price

1   Penetration price. This is the technique whereby the company enters the market at a price lower than that of the competition in order to win market share. It is mostly used in markets where there is little brand loyalty and customers are highly responsive to price moves. It is particularly advantageous when a new entrant develops a technological breakthrough, is able to offer output profitably at 10% below competition price, and so forces the less cost-effective companies out of the market. It is, however, a poor technique when used in markets with high brand loyalty or where considerable technological knowledge is applied, for it tends to compel reciprocal action and the net result is depressed prices with no one materially better off.

2   Skimming price. In the use of this technique the company concerned is endeavouring to up-market its product so as to improve further on quality, service and expenditure on marketing costs, and thus capitalise on its efforts. There is sufficient evidence to show that companies with high price tags ride the storms of depression more easily than cut-price merchants, mainly because the additional margin gives them more room to manoeuvre.

3   Competitive price. This is the common price around which most firms tend to bunch their quotes. It is frequently a cost-plus based estimate and tends to be used in fairly large stable markets. In such markets it is usually possible to make reasonably accurate sales estimates.

4   Diversionary price. The true price of products is not easily calculated because it is hidden by additional charges for extra necessary services. An example may be wall-to-wall carpeting in the home or a turnkey operation in industry.

5 *Dumping price* This is a process by which the supplying company offers products at a price 'below cost' but which, because of the marginal revenue/cost concepts, allows the company involved to make additional profits. The term usually refers to overseas trading, but is just as applicable in the home market. The principle is often practised where the manufacturer has one really large account buying below cost and, because of the volume handled, higher profits are made on the balance of the business than would have been possible if that business had had to stand alone.

It is sometimes, though not always, the practice adopted to supply major retail outlets with 'own-label' products.

Pricing for profit
While most firms strive to achieve a specific percentage return on output, they often fail to recognise that they are in effect standardising their opportunities. Although in discussion the managers concerned would agree that each product in the range requires a different investment in marketing costs, they nevertheless, in practice, allow all products to carry an equal absorption rate. This is a dissipation of effort. Some products supported by concentrated marketing effort could be sold at higher prices and at greater volume, while other products would not change in sales volume if no more than 1p were spent on promoting them. So while one product is ripe for exploitation and another already fully exploited, they still get an even amount of effort both in expenditure and in activity. This is a waste of company resources. And it is the major area where improved productivity in marketing is necessary and likely. Because it dictates the company's product mix policy, it is a key area for improvement in profitability. Although the pricing factor is a significant consideration, it is secondary to understanding the customer—a prerequisite of marketing orientation. It is the essence of product planning and pricing.

5 Marketing Planning

Marketing planning begins with the determination of marketing goals and develops through consideration of how these goals may be achieved. As a number of alternative courses will always be open to management, it is necessary for information to be obtained so as to aid problem-solving and ease decision-making. In this way planning is concerned with formalising management aspirations and with the quantity and the quality of effort needed to satisfy these ambitions. It is also involved with the company's ability to generate the necessary effort from all available resources.

Marketing planning shares with the other activities of the marketing mix the distinction in commerce of being a dynamic element in the business operation. Planning is dynamic because it provides a compulsive force; *it compels*:

1   The determination of real goals.
2   The exploration of different markets and the latent potential necessary to achieve real goals.
3   The systematic evaluation of the different product ideas needed in those markets.
4   A choice of marketing strategy appropriate to achieve anticipated market sales potential.
5   The consideration of the best type of organisation to exploit the situation.
6   The adoption of a monitoring system relevant to the chosen commercial operation.

This compulsive force indicates the real and lasting value of

the modern planning process; the true benefits of planning
come from the purely conceptual and mechanical effort needed
to establish and maintain a plan. The thinking through of
problems and the fullest consideration of the management
consequences following the introduction of any of the different
remedial measures available provide the basis for success. In
planning, the rewards come from what is put into the plan
rather than from what is eventually published.

The role of government in planning

Both government on the one hand and industry, trade and
commerce on the other each have a leading role in forecasting
and in the decision-making necessary for acceptable planning.
In Europe there is disagreement about the benefits or otherwise
of formal planning. The French are convinced planners and
believe that governments should set growth rates and investment targets for each industry, together with a national economic growth rate. These plans are co-ordinated through
committees of business, trade unions and government officials.
The German view, however, is quite different. They say that
the French are simply adding up opinions and that, no matter
what sophistication is used, it is not possible to produce
reliable figures by totalling personal views. They refuse to
accept that a sum of qualitative statements makes a quantitative realistic target. But the Germans do accept the need for
planning, although arguing that forecasts should be considered
no more than indicative.

In the UK the two leading political parties are credited with
contrasting beliefs, one believing in a planned economy and
the other in a free economy. The truth would show both
parties somewhere between these parameters, with neither
wishing to adopt, completely, an extreme doctrine. All British
governments in recent years have set themselves clear policy
objectives: the maintenance of full employment, satisfactory
balance of payments, reasonable price stability and a minimum

economic growth. In essence they have taken as their first priority the task of controlling the overall level of demand in the economy. The second task of government has been to encourage the full play of competitive forces. The Monopolies Commission and the Restrictive Practices Court are the vehicles for the implementation of parliamentary policies in this respect.

The nature and purpose of central planning

In the modern world most of the advanced nations have mixed economies, often with government spending in significant proportions. In order to obtain the funds necessary to carry out its programme every government must maintain taxation, with revenue coming from individuals and corporations alike. Moreover, as essential services are often provided by public corporations such as the Post Office, these provide each government with considerable economic power and influence. As the larger part of manufacturing industry and commerce is governed by economic market forces, it does not automatically follow that long-term, nor short-term for that matter, national needs are being met. So the government intervenes and encourages the redirection of industry and the redeployment of resources. Equally, the forces comprising the market economy do not always work quickly enough to avoid violent swings in demand, so the government tries to provide a stabilising force and to control fluctuations within desirable limits.

Because the nation enjoys the benefits accruing from economies of scale, investment decisions in new productive units, often involving substantials sums, need to be taken well in advance of actual demand. Because idle plant can mean considerable losses, firms tend to delay decisions as long as possible. So government aid and subsidies are used to encourage early investment, thus trying to avoid the 'stop/go' consequences.

The British government attempts to encourage competition

by reinforcing legislation against monopolies and restrictive practices. Moreover various Companies' Acts have been used to improve the quality of information provided in company accounts. Subsidies and incentives to industry are used to encourage a redistribution of industry, particularly in the development regions where resources lie fallow.

The growth in trading and the further development of industry and commerce necessitates the parallel expansion of services such as telecommunications, motorways, and port and harbour facilities. It is the government's adopted task to provide the satisfactory co-ordination of these needs.

Yet because the growth figures suggested proved unrealistic, the British National Plan of 1964 was discredited and finally discarded. It has since been suggested that the Plan could not succeed because it reminded the nation of wartime planning and was reminiscent of rationing and shortage. Such is the nature of things. The need for central planning, however, still exists, whether welcome or not.

Economic planning

Businesses have always planned in some way, and today this is almost a necessity. The increasing concentration of industrial units, resulting in a greater average unit size, has meant increasing complexity in decision-making. No longer is it possible in a big organisation for one man to absorb all the necessary intimate operational details of the enterprise and to exercise judgment on matters of the future. Decisions are not only complex, they often involve considerable sums of money, and influences may run for long periods well into the future. As companies now operate internationally, the complexity of operation is increased. So if resources are to be used efficiently and effectively, well-formulated specific plans are necessary.

Another significant justification for forward planning is in the increasing tempo of the rate of change—innovations in technology and socio-economic sectors. The amount of money spent on research and development alone justifies planning of expenditure and the return on investment possibilities in terms of resource allocation.

This is considered so important that the use of staff specialists can be supported, for line staff tend to be concerned with today's problems and may not be able to adapt their thinking to future needs. Nevertheless, co-operation with line staff is essential, otherwise direct contact with the market will be lost and many real issues missed. Also, line staff are responsible for implementation, so their involvement is critical. However, the impetus for policy-forming aspects of planning are top management's responsibility, leaving the detailed features to operational management.

Long-range planning

The only observation about history that is irrefutable is that change has been certain. Adaptation to environmental conditions was the basis of Darwin's theory of natural selection. What is most startling in today's environment is the actual *rate* of change. This century has seen more change than has occurred before in the entire history of the world. Certainly we can predict that the future will be unlike the past, that it will escape all imaginative prophesies and that the velocity of change will continue to increase.

In management terms this means that skills will fall behind the development of techniques and that the techniques will drag behind the advance in the complexity of problems. The only way these problems can be met is by improvements in the quality of decision-making. And that means better data.

It means that critical decisions have to be identified and the minimum level of decision-making information determined, and that level will often be decided statistically according to probability theory, with the level of risk in each decision premeditated and chanced.

In addition, there is a need for productivity increases in marketing management, particularly in the selling of capital goods. Forceful marketing of plant and machinery should spark off further increases in the productivity of consumer goods, and a rise in the standard of living. Increased productivity in the marketing function presupposes advances in the utilisation of marketing resources, so a greater need for planning is proved. Consumer needs will grow, markets will continue to expand, purchasing power will inflate, and capital, social and political expenditure will continue to develop. The firms that will benefit will be those that see ahead, make plans and exploit the opportunities. Planning as a management activity is here to stay.

Demand forecasting

Demand or sales forecasting is the raw material of the marketing plan. The sales budget, and from it the marketing budget, are developed from the forecast, which is the key to the whole comprehensive budgeting and planning process. From the sales forecast the company develops a number of related forecasts, plans and budgets which determine production plans and inventory plans, and, as such, the level of business activity. In this way it provides the supporting sales data for the company profit objectives, the capital budget and operational financial planning, including the actual cash flow.

Demand forecasting operates at three distinct levels:

1 Macro-economic forecasts
2 Industry forecasts
3 Micro-economic forecasts

Macro-economic forecasting is concerned with general economic conditions. In the developed economies it is usually related to some tied indicator of industrial production or national income and expenditure. It is the area of demand in which the ruling government takes more than a passive interest. Governments also take an interest in the level of industrial demand.

In the affluent countries it has been found that manipulating the fortunes of the car industry enables the politician to redirect the normal expenditure patterns of the population. For example, varying the initial deposit needed for a car purchase and changing the pay-back period enables the government to curb or stimulate consumer expenditure. By raising the value of the deposit and shortening the hire purchase period, the government slows down car consumption. As a result, the released disposable income each week is then spent on cash purchases such as clothes.

Intervention into the industrial evolutionary process is considered by many industrialists to be the root of British economic stagnation. By subsidising continuing investment in the old industries such as steel, coal and shipbuilding, the politicians have preserved votes but lost the opportunity to channel funds into those industries of the future, such as electronics, information, materials and leisure. It is no surprise that British industry finds it almost impossible to compete internationally in the competitively priced technological mass markets. The country may lead the world in the development and the production of major capital items such as turbines or nuclear reactors, but in the marketing of its produce it tends to lag behind, although more in reputation than in fact.

Demand or sales forecasting techniques

However, it is in forecasting at the level of the firm that the executive is mainly concerned. The forecast is a prediction of the level of sales activity if the circumstances remain unchanged, while the sales budget is the expected sales performance which the company sets as an objective. The budgeted figure may be set by management after allowance has been made for the effect of some additional factor over which the company can exercise influence, such as product quality or marketing expenditure.

The period for forecasts is wholly related to the lifespan of a product. Sales forecasts for repeat-selling consumer products such as frozen peas may only be prepared for one year ahead, in detail, while in shipbuilding a suitable period may be twenty years. But even this is not the whole truth, for in the world of fashion a particular style, as opposed to the garment itself, may survive for one short season only. Equally, a particular computer may be considered to provide a long period of service once installed, yet it may be obsolescent before installation is complete.

Short-term forecasting may often be undertaken using informed judgment and experience. Longer forecasts, often less liable to short fluctuations, lend themselves more readily to statistical projections. What does invalidate the universal acceptance of either method is the unpredictable nature of changing patterns of consumption. And therein lies the problem, for a demand function may only be possible if the sales determinants are constant, both during the period of observation and during the time of the forecast. For example, in short-term forecasting it is necessary to establish the conversion factors between determinants and the time-lag between each determinant as it functions.

£ooo's	Jan.	Feb.	Mar.	April	May	June	July	
	24	36	48	36	36	42	24	ENQUIRIES
	20	20	30	40	30	40	35	QUOTES
	20	10	10	15	20	15	20	ORDERS
	12	16	8	8	12	16	12	SALES

In this example of an early warning device there is a time-lag of three months between receipt of an enquiry and completion of a sale. The conversion ratios are 6:5 enquiries/quotes; 2:1 quotes/orders; 5:4 orders/sales. In essence if enquiries in March fall to 24 and there is no discernible change in time-lag or in conversion ratios, then the company concerned may expect sales to drop to 8 in June, subject to any remedial action being taken as a result of the warning highlighted.

The problem facing most firms in compiling such a method is in the spread of activities. Too many products, too many markets and inadequate manpower prohibit adequate preparation of a forecast. The solution is in isolating the significant products and the important markets—there will normally be few of these—and in preparing forecasts based on discernible trends and knowledge of market forces.

Developing the sales forecast

The method has many deviations inherent in its sequence, but some guide as to the steps necessary is essential.

Preliminary assessment
1 Level of profit assessment based on capital employed. How much profit is needed to meet obligations to shareholders and providers of loan capital?
2 The amount of sales volume needed to realise that profit figure.
3 The number and value of orders necessary for the sales volume to be achieved.
4 The number and value of quotations or tenders to be sent out in an effort to achieve the required level of orders.
5 The number and value of enquiries which have to be generated to provide for the quotations to be submitted.
6 The establishment of the conversion ratio or a trend in conversion ratio for each product group against required levels of profits, sales, orders, quotes and enquiries.
7 The measurement of the time-lag or a trend in the time-lag for each product group against required levels of profits etc.

This is a fairly simple method useful for the small business, which assumes that there is considerable market opportunity untapped. However, for the larger company this may not be realistic, because although it provides the manager with all the information he will need to develop his selling organisation it does not account for actual trends in the market place. In tackling this problem the manager has to use his best form of market feedback, the salesmen. Salesmen are usually asked to develop a sales forecast for their territory. The instructions given to them may involve the following steps:

1. Visit major accounts on territory (they probably account for 80% of his volume, although only 20% of his total customers at most) and get some positive idea of their future buying needs.
2. Check this information against recent data on buying and establish information consistent with trends.
3. Verify with customers where discrepancies arise.
4. With help of the manager apply confidence factors to each account forecast.
5. Remove from historical sales figures the actual volume achieved by these significant accounts.
6. Measure trends in the two separate sections.
7. Consider what action could improve the trends revealed.
8. What would it cost and is it worth it?
9. Arrive at figures consistent with trends in the market place and the costs of exploiting them.

Although these methods are the usual approaches adopted at the operational level, it is essential that the company prepares forecasts into the long term—not only for new products which themselves could alter the figures suggested by the sales force, but also for the development of new markets in anticipation of the decline of established markets. A staff officer would normally carry out such a procedure. He would evaluate prevailing and countervailing forces, such as:

1. Population trends
2. Developing living standards
3. Competition
4. World events

 5 Government policies
 6 Social values
 7 Psychological needs
 8 Fashions
 9 Seasonal factors
10 Technological change

Following an evaluation of these factors, the staff officer is in a position to develop the information into demand determinants.

Demand determinants

This is a relatively elementary approach to the problem of forecasting, but discovering the influences on conversion ratios between determinants and related time-lags often provides invaluable insight into the workings of the company's demand function. Apart from the activities of the sales force (see Chapter 9), demand determinants are:

1 The number of actual and potential buyers.
2 The available spending power of all buyers.
3 The influence of price in the market place.
4 The influence of pricing on substitutes.
5 The distribution of spending power.
6 The expectation of prosperity among consumers.
7 The established reputation of suppliers.
8 The structure of the industry.

As reliable quantitative analysis cannot normally be extracted from this mix because it is constantly changing, it is therefore necessary to apply unsophisticated weightings to each determinant. These may be varied as time suggests. But in the end they are no more than indicative and should never be used as ultimate proof for a forecast. Establishing a trend may be taken as more reliable, but causation factors need to be appraised before conclusions are drawn.

Long-term forecasting

Statistical techniques such as time series or multiple regression analysis are most often used because they tend to eliminate the influences of short-term variations. However, these techniques cannot be used in an industry liable to sudden and rapid change. Such industries are those that are long established and traditional in outlook. One such industry is the furniture trade. The signs for change are clear. Antique furniture is fashionable, as are Scandinavian designs—indications perhaps of searching for something better. Prophesying in the industry is fraught with danger, yet its members must do just that. They must consider what is influencing society today that will provide the industry with opportunities tomorrow. A pressing social problem is the shortage of living space, hence the dramatic increase in house prices. Yet each householder wastes space. Each room in every house is in use for a minor portion of each twenty-four-hour day. Apart from structural alterations it is furniture that provides the means by which 'general purpose' rooms could evolve. Furthermore, there is an alternative to structures. Housing associations are making houses available to people prepared to share certain basic services. Residential caravans and houseboats are appearing on farm land and on waterways. All these changes demand a new approach to furniture design. And the market is ready. So many teenagers leave home and move to the big cities, sharing with three or four others of their own age, that adaptable furnishings are an acceptable means to an end. Any erstwhile furniture designer should visit the bedsitter kingdoms of any big city and see expediency at work.

The financial control of marketing planning

The common denominator of business is money. By using money as a yardstick it is possible to make comparisons of uncomparable activities. Whatever the social ethics involved, we compare a train driver responsible for hundreds of lives with bookies by the amount of money society allows them. There is no direct comparison between their work, but we can compare them through the one factor common to them both—income, expressed in money terms. It may not be entirely satisfactory but it is workable.

This is also true in principle of marketing planning. No matter how unsatisfactory the system, we can compare relative values by the price society puts on them. So, despite assertions to the contrary, it is possible for the sales manager to prepare a comparison between recruiting a new salesman and spending more money on advertising. Once the common denominator is established it is then essential for the valuation of competing claims.

Marketing planning is in itself a financial control system. Suitably synthesised, the criteria is always: what is the return on investment consistent with the benefits of planning?

The benefits of marketing planning

Those companies that have successfully applied planning concepts have shown that the planning procedures involved lead to synergy: the practice brings greater total effectiveness than the sum of the separate parts would indicate. The major benefits at a company level are:

1 Considered judgment
2 Minimisation of capital requirements
3 Limiting of operating expenses
4 Optimisation of resources
5 Use of contribution analysis
6 Co-ordination of effort
7 Increasing personal responsibility
8 Internal competitive economies

These benefits are so important that some consideration of them is necessary.

1 Considered judgment
The only practical time to make unfavourable decisions is at a time of optimism when plans are first being made and tension is absent. Decisions forced on executives during periods of adverse trading conditions often produce emotive directions. Planning well in advance helps to ensure well-balanced considered judgment.

2 Minimisation of capital requirements
While planning may help to make more effective use of plant and machinery, it is most likely to provide better financial management and so it limits unrealistic demands for capital to finance expansion.

3 Limiting of operating expenses
It may also help to reduce working capital by the reduction of stocks and the control of debtors' credit through cash-flow policies. It should help also to make marketing expenditure more productive.

4 Optimisation of resources
By aiding decision-making the planning process reduces the incidence of business risk and so helps to bring a better return on invested capital.

5 Use of contribution analysis
By analysing the business and its component activities it is possible to provide rudimentary product costings from which arbitrary profit figures per product and per unit of output may be calculated. Some companies load overheads onto these figures or put absorption rates against their direct costs. The resultant figures may be misleading (see Chapter 3 on product planning and pricing), so a profit contribution figure is most likely to be reliable.

6 Co-ordination of effort

In writing his part of the plan the executive manager will discuss his plans with colleagues to get the best results. In establishing the objectives and budgeting the marketing mix a co-ordinated campaign plan will result. As every executive will know the programme of his colleagues, he will be able to fit into the overall pattern of activity that much better.

7 Increasing personal responsibility

Because remedial decisions are made prior to the event it is possible for junior executives to implement the necessary action at a predetermined level of activity. This amounts to day-to-day delegation of operational control, so making it possible for middle management to control significant management activities. In effect it is a substantial raising of the average level of responsibility in the firm.

8 Internal competitive economies

Individuals tend to associate themselves formally or informally with groups. Under sound management, employees endeavour to express their pride in collective achievement by attempting to improve on the performance of friends in other departments. Although these competitive activities may be beyond normal comparison, the common denominator of the budget provides the means by which measurement becomes possible.

The job of the planning manager

The planning manager is normally responsible to the marketing director for ensuring that the tasks of suggesting strategies of development, providing information, monitoring and recommending corrective courses of action for the company as a whole are successfully carried out. He will usually be responsible for the organisation of planning so that a basis for decision-making is possible. He will need to ensure a reservoir of knowledge is built up among his staff so that an appropriate perspective will evolve in operating departments. As these plans will need integration, it is essential that both planning and operational departments suggest ideas and act as a check on the contributions from others.

The person leading the planning department must be capable of operating at a level of abstraction. So he should have reached the stage of managerial maturity where he has the capacity to bear the uncertainty and anxiety of decision-making when the outcome is well into the future. He will thus have graduated from a performer to a thinker and planner. In order to make this transition satisfactorily he must have developed considerable marketing skills and be sufficiently numerate to apply quantitative techniques to planning problems.

The requirements of a plan

To be successful a plan must be organised into an agreed framework. A general format for a marketing plan is shown later. The essential requirements for a plan are:

1   It must have an objective.
2   It must be expressed in simple terms.
3   It must provide for measurement.
4   It must provide for contingencies.
5   It must make effective use of resources.
6   It must have a common denominator.
7   It must specify responsibility.
8   It must contain target completion dates.
9   It must include departmental activity tags.
10 It must inspire action.

The organisation of planning, following these simple rules, then becomes an integral part of the business. The practice of planning needs to be an essential ingredient in the work programme of the business executive, a way of business life, as natural and essential as the planning and organisation now taken for granted in a moon shot. In something as new as space exploration every conceivable influential factor has to be taken into account; no presuppositions are allowed to dominate without supporting data or information. Where chances are taken because of lack of information, then the risk is known, measured and allowed in the overriding decision that follows.

Once the plan is completed it becomes a vital working tool, a day-by-day standby for operational detail, support and guidance. Moreover, it is a record of pre-thinking, of operational activity and of post mortem.

Stages in the development of an operational marketing plan

To formulate a marketing plan properly it is necessary to go through a number of distinct but interdependent stages. Furthermore, within each of these steps there are a number of critical questions needing resolution.

The stages in the development of the marketing plan are:

	1	Corporate objectives.
	2	Overall marketing objectives.
Information	3	Audit of company resources.
	4	Marketing audit of company.
	5	Marketing environment analysis.
Analysis	6	Commercial analysis of individual products and/or services.
	7	Product range mix analysis.
	8	Identification of marketing objectives.
Decision	9	Establishment of marketing targets
	10	Determination of optimum organisation structures and scale of operation necessary.
	11	Development of appropriate marketing mix to meet objectives.
Action	12	The marketing plan.

The tools to be used in marketing planning are marketing research, which runs quite clearly through the whole planning process, and comparative cost analysis. The third critical tool is the analysis of the effectiveness of marketing methods. Together these tools make the planning process an instrument critical to commercial success by compelling the company to check all the possible ways of improving profitability, enabling it to react promptly and efficiently to all changes thought likely to influence its marketing activities.

The contents of the marketing plan

Following the pattern of development just described it is possible to prepare the marketing plan in a logical order. The actual measures that will comprise the plan are:

1. Development of objectives
2. Preparation of the sales forecast
3. Appraisal of competitor profiles
4. Analysis of market shares
5. Control of distribution
6. Schedule of publicity
7. Organisation of personnel
8. Arrangement of budgets
9. Provision of contingencies
10. Realisation of plans

(For a full consideration of these stages, see the author's book *How to Prepare a Marketing Plan*.)

Once these sections have been completed the company has created its operational manual. It is the manual that specifies action under every conceivable influence or happening. It is a full record of the thinking and the decisions, and the basis upon which they were arrived at, of the entire present and future operation of the company.

Contingency planning

No matter how carefully a company may have planned, something will go wrong and objectives will not be achieved. Planning is no panacea for commercial and industrial ills, so while it will often highlight problems and help towards their resolution it will not eliminate them altogether. Plans are made by people and they will make the plans according to their own judgment. This is often at fault. So the prudent introduce into the plan alternative courses of action. These will be in two sections. The first will contain the short-term action required to minimise or maximise possible consequences of deviations from plan, and the second the medium- to long-term action necessary to exploit the changed environment.

As it is not possible to predict exactly every likely significant event, the contingency plan will contain remedial actions against groups of consequences of unexpected occurrences. So the profit plan will show statements for 70%, 80%, 90% 110% and 120% actual performances against budget, each of these statements showing operational detail and headcounts. Automatically, at the time a trend becomes apparent at any one of these levels, prepared action takes place. This action will be to counter the adverse or the favourable position. It is a standby until such time as the cause for the variance is investigated and established.

The object of this short-term action is twofold: it is to preserve net profit and to secure future net profit. As profit has a higher incidence in the last 15% to 20% of sales, after overheads have been covered and when costs have become marginal, it follows almost by definition that a drop in sales will cause a more than proportionate decrease in profits. So in many instances preservation of sales performances must be taken as high priority in a contingency plan. Moreover, at the time the plan is established, each executive will have applied a sensitivity analysis to each item sufficient to question its viability at each level of operation. To this analysis will be applied the manager's own confidence factor. Confidence factors are the levels of expectancy that the man responsible applies to his targets. The principle is similar to that applied by bookmakers, who issue odds as a representation of their and their customers' joint evaluation of a horse's prospects. In purely commercial terms it is practised by assurance companies, who value premiums as confidence factors against death at a particular age group.

The marketing plan is a document of the corporate mind. It brings together all the separate parts, co-ordinates individual aspirations, both tethers and motivates as necessary, and conditions the collective minds of the organisation into the channels chosen for it by its leaders. In a way it can be regarded as an autobiography written prior to the period of its corporate life.

6 Distribution in Marketing

The process of distribution is not confined to the physical transportation of goods from manufacturer to consumer. The means by which a manufacturer makes goods available to his markets is a fundamental part of marketing strategy. Traditionally, consumers buy their requirements from a retail outlet, relying on their own judgment and that of the retailer in order to obtain best value for their money. This is becoming less true since sources of supply open to the individual are constantly changing. There has been, over the years, a major revolution in the channels of distribution affecting many familiar products.

Instead of selling automatically to retailers via wholesalers, companies are now considering the alternative ways in which they may bring their products to the attention of the public, making it convenient for people to buy at the most economical price. Certainly it is in the choice of distribution and the control of distribution that many companies have established their marketing reputations. Wimpy Bars, Macfisheries, Corona, Tupperware, Avon and Duckhams are well-known examples.

Manufacturers that at one time could supply only to wholesalers now use other means of distribution, even where they actually compete with wholesalers, and even retailers, for business. Wholesalers have always bought in bulk from manufacturers, specialising in a particular trade and selling goods in convenient quantities to retailers within their locality. The wholesaler earns a profit through bulk purchasing and prompt payment. In return he warehouses goods until required, sells and delivers, turning goods over as rapidly as possible in order to maximise the return on his investment. The major advantage to the manufacturer of using a wholesaler is a reduction in his own distribution costs. Without the wholesaler it may be necessary to make hundreds of small-value deliveries to retailers. The manufacturer will need to keep account of such trade and collect debts. Because the wholesaler provides the same type of service to a number of manufacturers he can spread the cost of operating his service over a number of suppliers, so minimising the expense incurred. In practice those manufacturers that have carried out the wholesaling function themselves have not managed to economise in any way, and the only advantage in continuing to bypass the wholesaler is greater control over the selling effort. The main disadvantage of using wholesalers is that they have little incentive to promote the goods of any specific manufacturer.

The distributive trades

The structure of the retail industry is complex. Conventional outlets range from corner shops to large department stores and multiple retail chains. Smaller outlets are often one-man businesses, whereas the chain stores are usually public companies. Independent retailers specialise in highly personal service, often providing credit and free deliveries. They tend to carry small stocks of a wide variety of goods within their accepted trade and, of necessity, charge comparatively high prices. Their customers prefer the specialised and individual service they provide and are prepared to pay a premium price in order to get the service that suits their needs.

Discount stores are a relatively recent innovation, although the principle has been practised for many years in certain trades. In line with recent trends they provide a self-service operation with a minimum of personal customer service. Customers select the goods they want, pay cash and find their own transport. Discount stores are predominantly non-food outlets which rely on a high rate of stock turn. Their growth has accelerated since the elimination of resale price maintenance on almost all consumer goods.

In combating the power of supermarkets, independent retailers have grouped together to form voluntary chains. As a group they arrange with wholesalers, and sometimes with manufacturers, to purchase in bulk, each outlet agreeing to take a specific share of the goods ordered.

Wholesaling

Recent changes in distribution patterns have reduced the volume of trade handled by wholesalers relative to other distributors and other channels of distribution. The wholesaling function takes many forms. It may be a specialist one handling a wide range of goods within a confined market group, such as pharmaceutical goods, or a general wholesaler who will carry those goods with a required profit margin irrespective of any market segment. Despite their decline in importance—due primarily to the disappearance of so many corner shops and the arrival of self-service on a large scale—wholesalers still provide a vital distributive function. The firm will buy in bulk and sell in small units, so reducing the incidence of physical distribution costs to the manufacturer. The wholesaler carries stocks and so provides a better back-up service to retailers, enabling the manufacturer to concentrate on economic batch production. And because the concern wholesales a wide range of goods, meeting the retailer's every requirement, more economic use is made of transport resources. Furthermore, wholesalers provide working capital to retail outlets in extending credit. However, for the growing manufacturer, the passive selling approach often adopted by wholesalers is inadequate. So he has moved away from selling through wholesalers and now controls his own selling effort by going direct to retailers, and in some cases direct to the consumer or user.

Supermarkets

The supermarket is probably the most significant innovation in retailing that has taken place in the past thirty years. A self-service store of more than 2000 square feet with a minimum of three check-out points, the supermarket specialises in the repeat selling of goods that are advertised nationally and for which there is a high regular demand. Because operators buy direct from manufacturers they are able to offer goods at low prices and to use cut prices and special offers to stimulate trade. Invariably they carry high fixed costs, and although the labour content is low, so is the profit margin per item sold. Thus supermarkets tend to measure profitability in terms of £'s per square foot of space rather than per item, although volume of sales for each product is an integral part of space costings.

Department stores

Department stores carry a wide variety of merchandise under one roof, usually on several floors of a building with specific departments handling particular groups of goods. There is a high standard of personal service, often with credit terms and delivery facilities. These stores insist on a high standard of personnel and compete with others through skilled buying and centralised management control.

Co-operative societies

Co-operative societies have long been established and work on the principle of customer ownership. The stores provide goods to members and non-members, the profits accruing at the year-end being distributed to members according to the value of purchases during the period. The structure of co-operatives may resemble any of the other types of competing outlet, although the limited range of goods which many carry is often considered a deterrent to potential shoppers. A significant proportion of each society's purchases come from the Co-operative Wholesale Society, which tends to standardise on goods supplied, so limiting the individual appeal in any one area of store.

Multiple shops

Multiple shops are normally groups under central control which specialise in a particular class of products. Because they deal in a small range of goods they are able to respond quickly to changes in taste and fashion. They tend to standardise in their product ranges and offer goods at reasonable prices. Normally buying in bulk, they have been able to integrate the retail and wholesale functions. More recently, they have become increasingly owned by manufacturers, who use them as a captive outlet for their own merchandise.

Variety chain stores

Variety chain stores operate in a similar way to multiples but are not restricted to a small range of goods. They operate closely with manufacturers and are able to utilise the economies of scale.

Self-service concepts

The traditional outlets have been increasingly attacked by entirely new concepts in retailing. The self-service concept is now spreading through many non-food outlets. It is being met increasingly in garages; and the garages themselves are meeting competition from specialist stockists for major items in car-consumables such as tyres, batteries and exhaust systems. Other specialist shops such as fashion boutiques and health food stores are now commonplace. The Mothercare chain is today almost a national network.

Franchising

Franchise marketing operations are a feature of a large number of shopping centres. The Wimpy Bar, Kentucky Fried Chicken restaurants and the launderette are well established and are providing services that did not exist in the same way previously. They are based on the marketing distribution concept traditionally used in public houses and, in this century, in petrol filling stations.

Some retail outlets have evolved because increased demand has not been satisfactorily met by traditional means. For instance, travel agents, earning discounts provided by tour operators, airlines and transport companies, make full arrangements for the traveller, giving advice on routes, accommodation and amenities. Likewise, money shops have appeared, providing 'instant' funds to credit-worthy customers.

Even the multiples have adjusted to demand in the High Street. Many of the long-established chains such as Marks & Spencer, British Home Stores and Woolworths now provide food counters. Some supermarkets have hit back by providing self-service clothing and accessories departments. The Home and Wear section of Tesco is an example.

Own-labels

Self-service and demand-pull advertising has swung selling power away from the retailer into the hands of the manufacturer. While the retailer needs to develop outlet loyalty in his locality, the manufacturer wants to establish brand loyalty irrespective of outlet. Advertising to the home and self-selection methods benefit the manufacturer in the balance-of-power struggle. In an effort to combat the strength of the manufacturer at the point of sale, retailers have introduced their own brands, obtaining quality products from reliable manufacturers and selling them under the reputation they themselves have built up as retailers. There is no better example than St Michael of Marks & Spencer Ltd.

In line with the changes in actual structure of retail selling are new methods of distribution for established products. In some cases traditional channels have been used for entirely different goods. Van selling has long been established for such products as milk and coal; yet today bread is delivered door to door along with soft drinks and is carried by vans operated by the milkman, or in the case of Corona by its own fleet of self-employed subcontractors. A substantial portion of ice-cream sales now appear to be made through mobile ice-cream parlours. Every child knows the meaning of those ubiquitous chimes. More recently, mobile fish-and-chip friers have appeared and, judging by the trade they seem to be generating, are here to say. Vending machines are now being used for such diverse products as cosmetics, books and ready-packed meals, in conjunction with microwave ovens.

Direct selling, door-to-door, has long been a feature of community living. In recent years the scope has gone far beyond the traditional household brushes or the encyclopaedia hawkers. Most consumer durables have now been offered across the doorstep. Even the collapse of the Rolls-Razor Company, selling twin-tub washing machines and making the greatest initial impact, did not deter imitators. Selling carpeting direct to the home has recently become as acceptable as the selling of insurance. Double-glazing is almost invariably sold door-to-door, although often supported by press advertising and local exhibitions.

More recent developments in self-service have come from hypermarkets and out-of-town shopping centres. Hypermarkets are giant supermarkets offering a full range of consumer durables and providing extensive parking facilities. Out-of-town shopping centres may be free-standing permanent structures or a collection, often running into hundreds, of stalls offering a wide range of goods.

Perhaps the most significant impact in direct selling has been in cosmetics. Avon, the pioneers, are the market leaders in this form of selling, but more recently the operators have suffered much press criticism. At first there was a rush to copy the Avon-type selling system, but only one or two firms have survived. The most radical has been Holiday Magic with its pyramid selling operation.

Pyramid selling

Holiday Magic operates on a four-level distribution structure from a central warehouse. The most junior level is the sales girls, who are supplied with a demonstration kit, literature and basic training in return for a small investment. Using their kits the sales girls retail products by demonstration to varying numbers of prospects. The prospects are given a full facial demonstration and free advice on skin-care without obligation. The advice may be given in the home, at party-plan gatherings, at meetings of womens' clubs and institutes, or by arrangement with hairdressers, beauty parlours and boutiques. The technique of getting the prospect to try the product before a purchase is encouraged.

Sales girls are recruited from the multitude of housewives who are able to work hours according to their needs and so earn accordingly. The girls are all self-employed and earn commission according to a sliding scale ranging from 30% to 48% on sales.

The sales girls are supplied through an organiser who has been responsible for their recruitment and has organised their training through the company. The organiser is the first level of promotion for sales girls, although he or she may have entered the operation at this level by making the required investment. The organiser receives an overriding commission which will vary according to volume of sales by his team. Every organiser has the opportunity to become a master distributor, who buys stock direct from the central warehouse at 55% discount and distributes through his team of organisers and their teams of sales girls. The master distributor and the organiser receive a percentage royalty on the volume of any other master they sponsor into the organisation.

The top level in the structure is that of general distributor, a position that must be earned through performance as a master. To become a general distributor the master must buy himself out of his sponsor's organisation and at the same time find a replacement for himself in that organisation. He is allowed to take his existing organisation with him, for which he will receive a discount of 65% as opposed to the 55% as a master. The former general will receive a lump sum from the newly created general, a replacement plus a 1% perpetual commission on all business achieved by his one-time subordinate.

The major incentives apart from high financial rewards are that promotion is always decided by each member according to his wish and his achievements. Once at the top of the distributive organisation, the general will gain maximum benefit by encouraging the progress of everyone who works for him in the distribution network. There are no area limitations; each member may work locally, nationally or internationally as he or she wishes. He is, at all times, protected by the sponsorship inherent in the set-up. All financial commitments are tied up in stock and the administration involved is not excessive. The major protection against loss is through promotion. As most members start at the organiser or sales girl level, each additional investment comes from earnings.

The system fell into disrepute because too many executives concentrated on obtaining the rewards of recruitment rather than on building a distributive system. As a result the organisation became top heavy and many people were reported to have lost their savings. The system is now subject to Government control.

Party-plan selling

The original party-plan type of selling started, or at least pioneered, by Tupperware has progressed and now includes the sale of such products as wigs, jewellery and children's clothing. The agent encourages housewives to throw tea parties for friends, so providing the agent with the opportunity to demonstrate her wares and win orders.

Mail order

Equally significant in terms of impact but with a much higher degree of penetration into the consumer area is mail order. There are a number of reasons for the rapid growth of this form of distribution, notably convenience, economy, credit, better buying information, privacy and the provision for returning unsuitable goods. These are all inherent in the marketing plan of companies that specialise in selling through mail order.

Shopping at leisure during any convenient moment or whilst relaxing, without having to travel around a shopping centre and being able to compare competing commodities from adequate information summarised in the catalogue, is now a trading method welcomed throughout society, particularly by young mothers or working wives. In many cases customers have become dedicated 'window shoppers', thumbing through catalogues and developing ideas about future requirements. The system has allowed the consumer to have almost the equivalent of a department store in the home.

Causes of changes in distribution methods

In the development of a marketing plan a decision has to be made as to how customers are to be serviced. For example, in distributing a trade magazine it would be necessary to define the type and the number of readers required. So a profile would be developed of the desired reader and an effort made to ascertain the number in existence. Most often this problem is one for the manufacturer. The service organisations and the distributive trades have developed along traditional lines and their channels tend to be firmly established. And this is the main danger to such organisations, for during the past decade the changes in retail distributions have been such that a radical upheaval in retail trade management is necessary.

These changes are being brought about by three trends. First, the costs of distribution are increasing at a higher rate than ever before. And product-line policies involve an increasing variety of choices open to the consumer, while the consumer himself is experiencing a fundamental change in personal habits and social behaviour.

The costs of distribution have been a constant source of worry to economists and politicians alike for many years. It was said of the nineteenth century that its merchants had solved the problems of production and left the problems of distribution to the twentieth century. In effect this is true, for the industrial revolution provided the basis for today's mass-production techniques; yet these techniques are valueless in themselves unless the goods so produced can be sold. And therein lies the problem. Machines can be developed which operate at high speed and low cost, so reducing the unit production cost for their output. Yet distributing and selling is not easily subjected to automation. In fact, the tendency has always been towards artistic qualities in the marketing sphere, with a minimum of scientific application. In practical terms it seems that the initial output from a machine is comparatively easy to sell because it is bought by the well-to-do who would have been prepared to pay more. But as output is increased it is sold to people with a lower and lower level of funds and less propensity to buy. Each successful sale requires a marginally higher marketing cost, up to the point where incremental revenue equals incremental cost—the point of optimum profit. Now, in effect, this often means that the cost of distribution rises with the economies of scale, and it may eventually exceed the production and materials costs of the product. Yet if the distribution costs had not been incurred, the high level of sales would not have been achieved and the costs of manufacture could have been substantially higher, even to the point where they exceeded the combined costs of manufacture and distribution achieved when sold in volume and where incremental costs equalled incremental revenue.

One of the complaints frequently heard against the use of mass-production techniques is the elimination of choice that this involves. Well, clearly if mass marketing means mass production and together they mean goods at a price that can be afforded by all, then the elimination of choice for the minority may be a price worth paying, if in fact this were true. It is not, for the increasing variety of goods being made available is such that additional distribution costs have resulted.

Once mass markets have been established it becomes necessary for production to be increasingly concentrated at fewer and fewer locations. This standardisation of production points has two effects. First, it means that mass production can be achieved for a significant part of the total manufacturing process, so allowing an infinite variety of choice at the final assembly stage; and, secondly, it removes production from the immediate locality of markets and hence increases the physical distribution costs. And because of the considerable variety of completed goods held in stock by distributors and the administration costs of that stock handling, the channel distribution costs have increased as well.

In addition to this improvement in the variety of goods must be considered the extent to which the provision of convenience foods has increased distribution costs. Frozen foods have to be carried in refrigerated lorries and warehoused in cold-storage plants, and at the point of purchase they need a refrigerated display cabinet—all costs of distribution. Convenience foods provide an 'added value' to customers and this in itself is part of the service which has to be paid for in the distributive process.

But perhaps the most significant change in contributory factors has taken place in the market place itself. Modern society is living in an era of abundance; there is no real shortage of supply. Indeed, there is a surplus capacity in most countries, hence the unemployment figures. It has all come from productivity due to mass demand. And because there is no shortage the standard of living is high and relative values change. The shift towards leisure pursuits has ensured new markets for new industries and new markets for old industries. Time-saving and labour-saving devices and the elimination of drudgery and monotony in the domestic scene have altered the entire face of the average consumer. In fact, changes in the distribution of wealth have caused a major upheaval in the levels of demand and in the distributive channels that service them.

The organisation of distribution

In developing his organisation for marketing, the executive concerned must consider the type of outlet that will provide the selling point to the ultimate customer. For example, in selling books the publisher may choose a direct selling approach, with sales people calling at prospective customers' homes. Or he may decide on a vending machine sited at a railway station. Similarly, his choice may range through booksellers, mail order firms or book clubs. He may even elect to have his books distributed by a special class of outlet, such as a hairdresser, a boutique or a chemist's. This decision-making process is also true of the industrial equipment company, which makes a similar evaluation of alternatives.

In his assessment the executive will consider a number of influential factors. For instance, if he uses an agent in an overseas territory and decides to evaluate a possible alternative, such as establishing a branch office with his own employees, he will need to consider the conflicting merits of the following:

1 Product technicalities
2 Local channels of distribution
3 The actual market size and potential
4 The level of service needed
5 The after-sales service provided
6 Language problems
7 Nationalistic attitudes
8 Size and geography of territory
9 Availability of staff
10 Competitive pressures
11 Distance from headquarters
12 Co-operation of agent

13 Government regulations
14 Identifying consumers
15 Operating costs

Although from the manufacturer's point of view the major considerations in distribution are time and cost, the long-term development of a business is often a short-term problem. Detailed consideration of these commercial factors is, therefore, of paramount importance.

Product technicalities
Highly technical products tend to be sold by qualified technicians. While it is often enough for the seller to understand customer benefits, it is sometimes difficult for an unqualified man to win the confidence of a buyer, who invariably will be technically skilled. So instead of teaching salesmen to emphasise product qualities and to understand market needs, employers take the easy route and hire the engineer or the pharmacist according to the product characteristics. In a market area where this practice is common the employer will want to know the extent to which he is conforming or pioneering in his approach.

2 Local channels of distribution
Who you know, not what you know, is a value factor. Certain people, either through industry or through flair, have established valuable connections within particular trades. They may not be particularly knowledgeable but their contacts have confidence in them, usually built up over a long period, and their loyalty to such people amounts almost to restrictive practices. Yet this should be regarded by the manufacturer as 'brand loyalty' involving a certain degree of monopoly in the market place.

Such people and organisations are common in the distributive trades, and it takes great courage and foresight to bypass 'the trade'. It is certainly not desirable unless one is in a position to operate from strength. Internationally known and accepted products often carve their own path, under appropriate guidance, through trade channels. But knowing the existing channels of distribution is critical, whether one chooses to use them or not.

3 Market size and potential

Although there is much to be gained from entering an established and sizeable market, equally there are advantages in aiming at markets with growth potential. In an established market there will be much information available about prospects and needs. Equally, the demand will be matured and the selling activity devoted to influencing the selected alternatives, rather than to educating the market and building up demand. But an untapped market gives rapid growth opportunities from early penetration, often resulting in buyer loyalty.

Ideally, one should select a market with growth potential which seems to have reached a high-level plateau yet is still waiting to take off. Examples in the UK during the early part of the 1970s appear to be the leisure industry and off-shore exploration.

4 The level of service needed

Although many products are sold over the counter, there are just as many that are custom-built and require installation and servicing prior to use. This is certainly true of many consumer durables and almost invariably true of capital equipment. In either case there may be a need for demonstration or even instruction to users on the efficient use of the appliance. The level of service and the technical knowledge necessary to carry out that service will often dictate the type of organisation most suitable for the task.

5 Afer-sales service

Similarly, complex equipment needs regular maintenance and service, together with easily available spare parts. Many organisations have built up their business through using superior sales service and after-sales service as their major marketing strategy. The most notable example is provided by the Volkswagen Company of Germany, which introduced minimum standards of performance for its distributors as well as conformity in service standards for its agents' mechanics. It accounts for much of the success of the Beetle. As yet, after-sales service is under-utilised as a pre-order promotional activity at a corporate level. Yet salesmen often use the back-up service as a selling tool. It is perhaps unfortunate that many companies give a low priority to this aspect of their operation and thus are unwilling to draw attention to it. Companies have great opportunities to win business by improvements in this area.

6 Language problems

Communications between indigenous members of a population are difficult enough without the added complication of foreign languages. Yet foreign trade is a fact of life, and as no international language is totally acceptable it is up to the supplier to adapt to the needs of his customers and so speak their language.

While this is desirable at the personal level it is absolutely essential in literature, whether letters or promotional brochures. People do not buy something they do not understand and they will not accept an oral representation of a leaflet any more than you, the reader, would.

In countries where English, German or French is the native tongue the problem is usually easily surmountable. However, other languages do present obstacles, and unless bilingual specialists can be recruited it is often better to use specialist organisations rather than to set up a branch or a subsidiary.

7 Nationalistic attitudes

Many natives are uncompromisingly patriotic and refuse to consider any foreign alternatives to home-produced goods no matter how inferior the local goods may be. Between two different countries with common boundaries there may even be open hostility through centuries of dispute over territorial lines. Often an industry becomes almost totally dependent on another country for sales of its produce. The dairy produce trade from New Zealand to the UK is a prime example which aroused much passion during the UK entry negotiations with Common Market officials.

The UK itself has a similar dependence on Spain for the survival of its travel industry. The inclusive tour operators rely on Spain for a large percentage of their business. If Spain were to close its doors to the UK, for example over Gibraltar, then the industry in this country might well collapse almost overnight for a period. Spain would not suffer to the same extent because its surplus could easily be taken up by the German and French tourists, all with ample funds and unrestricted opportunity to enter the country.

Exporters from the UK have to be particularly careful, because so many overseas countries have attitudes towards the British running back many centuries.

8 Size and geography of territory

Belgium is often chosen by the world's exporters as the test market for overseas marketing. The country is geographically small and 25% of its population is located in the four cities of Antwerp, Brussels, Liege and Ghent.

Other countries, however, are not so easily penetrated. The General Manager of Lakes of Zambia Ltd, George A. Poulter, once gave a lift to a native and carried him 140 miles in his car to the nearest airport. On arrival the African, in awe, said he had not realised just how big Africa was; everything is relative! Geographically, some countries are impossible to tackle in one go. Ayala Designs built up its European business before tackling the logical, yet enormous, market in North America. Even then the company found it necessary to use a distributor with a national connection.

The terrain of some countries may prove a deterrent. Even in Europe there are some countries considered inaccessible. Communications in parts of Wales and Scotland are considered almost non-existent, while access or egress in Norway is impossible for much of the year.

9 Availability of staff
Most countries have their unemployed, yet the very skills most needed by the trader will be universally demanded and the availability of such persons strictly limited.

Often it is better to take the necessary personnel into the country where entry and work permits are possible, although this creates the language or nationalistic problem already mentioned.

10 Competitive pressures
The competition in every country will have decided its own marketing strategy, either as a result of a purposeful marketing plan or through expediency. The success or otherwise of these policies could be indicative of trends in the organisational structure of the distributive system native to the country concerned. Knowing the pricing policies of competitors enables a company to decide on its own entry point in the market and how much may have to be made available for distribution.

It is by assessing the needs of the market and by studying how the market is being served that a company carries out its 'gap analysis' and discovers just where the greatest potential is for its own approach.

The company may choose to isolate and to weight the bases of purchasing decisions by consumers or users. Normally a decision will involve consideration of:

(a) Price
(b) Technical specification
(c) Delivery and supporting services

    (*d*)   Packaging or packing
    (*e*)   Company reputation
    (*f*)   Product or service reputation
    (*g*)   Personal connection

The technical specification will include the quality and performance of the item concerned.

11 *Distance from headquarters*

One of the many disadvantages of using distributors is loss of effective control of the marketing effort. Distributors take on a product and, as often as not, hope it will catch on during the course of their normal promotional activities. If it does, then it may get more attention. If it does not, then it will be allowed to stagnate. Usually the product will get as much attention as the manufacturer demands and ensures of the distributor. This may often prove expensive in executive travel time.

Even in establishing a subsidiary or a branch office, it is essential to organise a proper monitoring system. Seeking regular reports, preferably according to a fixed schedule with predetermined reporting activities, is a vital means of effective control. Usually the further a branch is away from the head office, the more difficult it is to exercise such control.

So introducing and maintaining a full reporting system helps to ensure that the new venture grows up in the company image rather than as a wayward maverick.

12 *Co-operation of agent*

Often a reorganisation means loss of earnings to an agent. The manufacturer should recognise that this probability is not likely to excite the fullest co-operation when new plans are afoot.

If the co-operation of an agent is sought, and it is usually essential prior to the establishment of a local branch, then these services should be paid for in some way, even to the point of allowing the agent some future commission for his assistance. It needs to be recognised that, apart from simply bringing in orders, in the past the agent has been building up a business connection and that future sales may often be dependent on the foundations laid by the distributor. He may be equally useful in the future.

13 Government regulations

Apart from import restrictions, the biggest problem facing an importer will be in the safety regulations in the country of destination. The best source of information in the UK on this problem is THE—Technical Help for Exporters.

14 Identifying the consumer

If direct customer contact has always been left to the distributor it is not always easy for the manufacturer to develop a profile which will enable him to maintain his own direct contact in the market.

Agents are aware that successful importers may soon establish themselves in a growth market and that it is not always in their interest to reveal the secrets of their success or to allow the supplier access to customer lists. Knowing the customer enables the company to set up a suitable sales force and to develop a relevant advertising campaign using appropriate media.

15 Operating costs

This is easily the area most fraught with difficulty. Few companies really know just how much these costs are. The only way in which one can judge the feasibility of any distributive channel is by estimating profit contributions against likely volume. Because of the number of variables involved, a considerable degree of guesswork is inevitable no matter how sophisticated the accounting approach.

Often in practice it makes more sense for an importer to take over local companies, so ensuring that many of the initial induction problems are avoided. In 1966 Watneys had become a local brewer in Belgium by acquiring the 'top fermentation possibilities' of the Delbruyere Group near Charleroi, and then it bought and merged the Vandenheuvel Group in Brussels, followed by the Maes Concern in 1969; it then had an estimated 7% share of the substantial Belgian market.

Pricing decisions

Many manufacturers use a mixture of distribution channels. In some areas of the country they may sell direct to retailers, but in other areas where volume is low they are content to supply to one wholesaler. Similarly, in some channels it is worth while selling to a specialist wholesaler so as to get the most efficient national coverage. Furthermore, it often pays to let a rival concern have supplies of a product and to allow them to market it under their own brand name. Some manufacturers sell a product under two distinct names, one being sold through one channel and the other through another. Manufacturers use these maneouvres not merely to achieve extra volume or market share but because they are often able to inflict discrimination on prices or on discounts according to different channels.

Mass marketing, the offspring of distribution

One of the early attempts at effective distribution was created in the mid-nineteenth century with the birth of the co-operative movement. Today the movement is one of the largest, if not the most successful, of the distribution networks. But the basic idea behind the Co-operative Society is essentially a marketing concept. As a national organisation based on the original principle of shopkeeper/manufacturer it soon evolved into a manufacturer/wholesaler/branch shop network, just as we know it today. The principle of good value for money aimed at mass markets precipitated mass marketing in order to sell the bulk supplies bought at low prices.

Physical distribution

All forms of transport are used to transfer man or materials from one point to another. To have immediate access to a product improves its value. Transport provides access and therefore increases the value of goods to society. In this sense it is wrong to look on transportation merely as a cost, for in truth it is adding value to goods by improving their marketability. This improvement in the value of goods is just as important to the purchaser as would be an improvement in design or an increase in quantity. Fast, inexpensive and efficient transport provides one of the critical elements in the development of communications and hence the advancement of marketing processes during the past hundred years or so. A transport network is one of the predominant features of all developed societies and is one of the first priorities undertaken by all developing nations in the promotion of trade.

Effective transport is a vital part of modern affluence and productivity. The economies of scale would be impossible without the means of distributing goods throughout the length and breadth of the land where they are demanded. The major areas of consumption, the big cities, would not have evolved without transport. No city as big as London could possibly survive from its own output. The UK itself is a substantial importer of its foodstuffs and could not last for more than a few months without imports, hence the efforts to prevent convoys reaching the country during the last war and the need for the country to maintain an efficient navy throughout its history.

7 Publicity—1

Advertising is a distinguishing feature prominent in the everyday lives of people in a free economy. Advertising is a marketing tool which aims to gain attention and to be noticed. And because it does this so successfully and is so widespread, it is frequently considered the most powerful of the marketing activities. While it is true that advertising is powerful, it is nonetheless no more than a significant element in the marketing of a product, for marketing is a fully integrated discipline requiring a purposeful blend of marketing activities. Thus advertising may on occasion be the most powerful tool but only to achieve a predetermined objective or objectives within the framework of a co-ordinated campaign. As such it is complementary to other marketing tools. The actual blend of the marketing mix and part played by advertising has been given some consideration in Chapter 2.

Most non-marketing executives will be aware of the impact of advertising in the marketing of branded consumer goods because they, as consumers, constitute critical market targets, according to their spending power, and as such figure prominently in the promotional plans of some advertisers. Yet in their everyday business activities they tend to be isolated from the attention of the suppliers of goods and services. So they have little awareness of the advertising strategies employed by these promoters.

Repeat selling consumer goods

Advertising is a key promotional aid in the selling of goods that have a low unit price and are subject to frequent and constant consumption. Examples are foods, household necessities such as soap and detergents, toilet and cosmetic preparations, proprietary medicines and, until recently, cigarettes and tobacco. The principles involved in the marketing of these goods are relevant, however, to consumer durables and to industrial goods and services.

There are over eighteen million households in the UK and many hundreds of millions more in overseas markets. Multinational companies with scope for mass markets throughout the world need to ensure that markets in the industrially developed countries provide the sustained growth in demand and tempo which makes mass production and further development viable. To achieve this aim the producer must communicate with his customer through advertising. He must advertise continuously in order to win the confidence and co-operation of the trade, and the support of customers. The consuming public is daily making choices and so advertisers are concerned with an *ever-changing share of an ever-changing market*. So to ensure that changes are to their advantage advertisers must keep their names in front of the public. They must advertise regularly. The central themes behind every campaign must be *concentration*, *repetition*, and *domination*.

In order to sell successfully a product must give the consumer real satisfaction. It can only do this if it is good value for money, at least in the minds of the chosen market. So marketing men aim to obtain consumer goodwill. This brand loyalty, as it becomes, is built up from regular purchases. The function of advertising is to state the case for the product, to persuade people to try it and to remind those who have already tried it that it is there to be bought again. Products are therefore branded or carry the manufacturer's trade mark. This helps to ensure that a product is easily recognisable. It also brings to satisfied customers a form of guarantee that a further purchase will be of the same quality as the earlier one.

Many a product has been an established household word for many years. Often such products are heavily advertised. It may be concluded that such brands owe their success to advertising. Yet it would be more appropriate to say that advertising has brought the product to the attention of millions, over many years, and that as the product is still selling, and selling successfully, it has stood the test, repeatedly, of consumer satisfaction. It is not advertising that has made such products popular but the fact that they were sufficiently good to withstand critical market tests and thus make heavy expenditure on advertising worth while.

The services of an advertising agency

The very early advertising agencies were space salesmen, who sold their employer's advertising services by writing and designing clients' advertisements. These salesmen soon realised that advertisers needed more than one medium for their publicity, and so they became space brokers, earning commissions from the media-owners for placing advertisements. The commission system persists today, although it is often supplemented by service fees. The range of services offered by an agency, principally to make advertising campaigns more effective, is so comprehensive that commission, particularly on small budgets, does not cover the costs involved.

There are about 1000 advertising agencies in the UK of which a quarter are members of the Institute of Practitioners in Advertising. Agencies may consist of just a few highly skilled specialists or offer a total marketing service with hundreds of employees. A number of the larger agencies are able to undertake campaigns on an international scale, while smaller agencies often have good associations with a network of overseas agencies.

The primary function of the agency is to help the advertiser to sell his product as efficiently and as economically as possible. In order to do this the agency will suggest the appropriate use of media and will prepare campaign plans to achieve the company's objectives. But since advertising is only a part of the total promotional campaign, agencies need to make other services available for the use of clients. These services often include market research, packaging and display, merchandising and public relations. In recent years the agencies have formed separate operating companies to undertake these services. The administration and control is simplified in this way, particularly the question of payment.

Most advertising campaigns are no longer the result of inspired ideas created by brilliant individuals, although some creative hot-shops have established themselves recently, and it must be admitted some recent campaigns have been successful due to creative flair. However, the modern campaign is plotted and planned with considerable accuracy. It is brought about by the study of media. The media planners collect and evaluate the wealth of information made available by newspapers, the trade and technical press, television companies, the academic world, research companies and HM Stationery Office. The media planners are trying to discover the best media to use for particular campaigns and how to get the best out of the money available. So the media planning department deals with the problems of using the client's advertising appropriation to convey his advertising message to the selected market segment and to make the most effective impact upon that chosen audience. The media buying department then converts this campaign plan into the actual purchase of advertising space and time.

Supplementing this activity is the creative department. The creativity of an agency may often prove to be its most outstanding feature, for the department contains artistic and literary services, providing suitable typography, artwork, copy and scripts.

The marketing department of an agency links closely with

the client's own marketing department on such activities as pricing policies, trading terms, channel decisions, sales policies, market trends and competitive activity.

Deciding the advertising appropriation

Ideally, the advertising appropriation should be the minimum amount needed to achieve the company's marketing objectives. The objectives may relate to market share or to maintaining a premium price; they may even relate to establishing a chosen company image or perhaps to developing the total market for a product. It is the amount needed to achieve such objectives that dominates the total publicity budget, of which advertising plays a significant part. So the expenditure on advertising should be the most economical means of achieving the pre-set goals.

In practice the advertiser has a good idea of how much his advertising should cost for an established product. His experience of numerous campaigns, different media tried and various amounts of money expended will have given him, within narrow limits, a shrewd guide to the level of expenditure most suited to his needs. Perhaps one day a pre-set formula may become applicable, but the changing pattern of behaviour in consumer purchasing habits defies all attempts to establish criteria for evaluation. It is not possible to prophesy or to measure subsequently the effect advertising has on sales.

Launching a new product provides the advertisers with many almost insoluble problems: not only is the launch costly but also the risks are high. Before commercial television was introduced in the UK in 1956, a manufacturer had no means of carrying out a realistic test campaign in one area. Although he could use regional newspapers, the impact of national or Sunday papers would be missing. The area exercise would not therefore provide a sound indication of the success or otherwise of a national launch.

But commercial television with regional coverage made it

possible for test marketing to be undertaken. An effective marketing campaign, with advertising appearing in regional media, can now be launched in a single area on a scale that is pro-rata to the possible expenditure in a national effort. Often success in one region encourages the company to undertake a major effort paid, as it were, out of the confidence accumulated in the initial test. But frequently the most important benefit from an area launch is the lessons learned.

Not all companies, however, decide their advertising appropriation in this way. The most common methods, often using expected sales revenue as a determinant, are:

1 Fixed percentage on past sales
2 Fixed percentage on expected sales
3 Competitive parity
4 Predicted surplus

Each of these alternatives, however, has particular advantages and disadvantages.

1 Fixed percentage on past sales
As past sales are the sole determinant, the expenditure has little or no relevance to the current needs. It is particularly questionable in markets subject to rapid change. Its major advantage is that the money has already been earned and the question of being able to afford the amount does not arise.

2 Fixed percentage on expected sales
The major advantage which may, but does not always, result from this method is the incentive to improve sales forecasting attempts. It also means that costs can be predicted according to sales volume and therefore controlled within tolerable limits. The system does have the fundamental disadvantage of discounting influential factors and it is therefore possible to accelerate a slump unnecessarily.

3 Competitive parity
The sole advantage of this method is that it may pre-empt a

war between companies on the level of expenditure. The parity made would, however, have to have universal acceptance.

The system loses its relevance when it is considered that advertising is but one of the marketing tools and the blend of the marketing mix is unique to each company. Attempting to standardise on the rate of one element alone will cause distortion, for it will benefit some and injure others.

4 Predicted surplus

The system needs some explanation. A company calculates gross profit from its sales targets, deducts a satisfactory level of profit and then uses the surplus for advertising purposes.

While the system is an aid to profit orientation, it does pose problems as to what constitutes a satisfactory profit. It also means that where forecasts show a decline in revenue, unless advertising provides a boost, profit levels will almost certainly be maintained and advertising reduced.

Clearly none of these methods is entirely satisfactory, although the percentage to sales variation is probably the most often used. In the UK it has fluctuated around a national average of 3% of sales. All the methods described are dependent on the total advertising budget being set and then used as necessary. There is much justification for a new approach. Sales targets are set by sales region and based, ideally, on market sales potential. It should not be beyond the resources of the marketing man to build up a model for each territory using the same input as that employed in establishing sales targets aimed at achieving territorial objectives. These could then be totalled to arrive at the amount of the advertising appropriation. It is true that this presents problems in the UK, a country almost unique in its numerous national newspapers; but with the advent of commercial radio, allied to the growing influence of regional newspapers and free sheets, the possibility is real. Similar efforts could be applied to each brand or, perhaps, to each product group.

The advertising media

The various advertising media provide the manufacturer with almost infinite variety in communicating his message to the widest possible chosen audience. The UK is rich in the coverage and intensity of penetration of its media among consumers. The press is particularly impressive in this respect. The major categories are:

1 National dailies and Sundays
2 London evening papers
3 Weekly colour supplements
4 Provincial dailies and weeklies
5 Major consumer magazines
6 Trade, technical and professional press
7 Telephone directory yellow pages
8 Free sheets
9 Directories and annuals

Of particular significance is the trend towards providing data supplements. These are particularly useful to specific categories of readers, and because of the intense interest they arouse they bring increased traffic to the publication. The major advantages the press brings to the advertiser are selectivity, detail and some longevity. In terms of flexibility and therefore economy, the press is a significant advertising force and consumes the greater proportion of advertisers' annual expenditure.

Other advertising media are:

1 Independent television
2 Outdoor advertising
3 Commercial radio
4 Cinemas, theatres, bingo halls
5 Door-to-door distribution

6 Exhibitions

7 Films or filmstrips

Direct mail, sales promotion, merchandising, packaging and public relations are the other main publicity activities, and are covered later in this chapter and in Chapter 8. Some further consideration, however, of the listed media is warranted.

1 Independent television

Experience shows that television is the most powerful of the advertising media. It is partially responsible for the parallel advance in self-service trading and for the greater use of packaging technology and creative skills. It works its appeal while its audience is relaxed and receptive in their own homes. It combines visual appeal with persuasive tones and even jingles. It is possible to demonstrate a product, and occasionally one finds an advertising theme that makes an appeal to some deep-seated emotion such as the maternal instinct. Some advertisers have prepared their advertisements with such care that it is possible almost to *taste* the product advertised—think of 'succulent' Walls sausages—to *feel* the Macleans 'tingle' or to *smell* the 'fresh farm' of Kerrygold.

The medium is, however, expensive, particularly with colour, and it is only economic, subject to the aims of the individual advertiser, for repeat selling consumer goods, and perhaps consumer durables with universal appeal and, needless to say, reasonable margins. For these it is cost-effective.

2 Outdoor advertising

This group covers both posters and transportation advertising. It also includes neon signs. Posters are particularly useful to the advertiser because, by selecting the appropriate sign, he is able to appeal to a chosen audience, to provide repetition of the message and to monopolise an attractive position for the duration of his contract.

Transportation advertising incorporates all advertising in

public vehicles: trains, buses, the underground, Post Office vans, even taxis. It also includes posters in railway stations, bus stations, shelters and the underground escalators. Although transportation advertising is allied to outdoor advertising, it is advisable to keep the two separate for media comparison purposes. This form of advertising is most useful for reinforcing the impact of major campaigns, particularly where some critical message needs to be registered in customers' minds before action is taken. This is true, for example, of insurance, where the theme needs to be constantly in front of the consumer for penetration to be realised.

3 Commercial radio

Until 1973 commercial radio in the UK had been confined to Radio Luxembourg and to another overseas station which did not survive the last war. There had, in addition, been a number of pirate stations, such as Radio Caroline and Radio London, which showed the viability of commercial radio and also bred many of today's successful disc jockeys. Radio Meux and Radio Eireann survive today.

Commercial radio officially opened up in the UK in 1973 with the launching of Capital Radio and London Broadcasting. They will be followed by a network of stations throughout the country. As a medium, commercial radio will present its advertising message at a convenient time of the day for the product concerned and to preselected audiences; it is personalised, is capable of creative flexibility and so provides an invaluable support medium to television or the press. And it opens up new opportunities for local traders to promote their goods in competition with national concerns.

The success of commercial radio will, however, depend on its ability to attract revenue from the local advertisers. Equally important is the need to increase the total revenue for advertising by educating local businesses on the benefits to trade that advertising can bring. Simply winning revenue from the local press would be a wasted opportunity.

Perhaps the most compelling advantage of radio advertising is the possibilities it opens up for media planners to quantify more readily advertising effectiveness. At the moment there remains a sizeable gap in the communications network, sufficient to invalidate any hypothesis on total advertising.

4 Cinemas, theatres, bingo halls

These are useful to the advertiser because they attract particular audience categories. The cinema, for example, is considered the most powerful medium for appealing to young adults—there are almost fifteen million in this age group (16 to 34) and it includes a significant proportion of young marrieds with tremendous buying power and a critical purchasing period. It accounts for one third of the money-spending adults going through their most acquisitive period in setting up a home. Appeals are:

(a)   Use of colour
(b)   Large animated screen
(c)   Advertising limited to one time in programme
(d)   High attention value

5 Door-to-door distribution

The only really efficient sampling method, this has the advantages of selectivity of areas and 100% effective coverage of the total market. It is, however, extremely expensive. It is the major promotional device for leaflets of the voluntary groups such as MACE and VG. Many attempts have been made to build a regular network for samples through an established distribution force such as the postman or milkman. These have been unsuccessful, whereas some small private concerns have made a considerable impact using this method. The direct-to-consumer carpeting firms or deep-freeze specialists distribute leaflets through a chain of local housewives, with salesmen following up any leads that result.

6 *Exhibitions*

The exhibition as a means of marketing promotion has yet to win the acclaim it deserves. In many cases the exhibition or trade fair is the only means by which the total market can be filtered and prospects uncovered economically worldwide.

For the salesman exhibitions offer an opportunity to substantially increase his productivity, because not only are his customers coming to him but he also does not have to worry about travelling time or waiting time. Every minute is selling time. But to ensure that the time is well spent, each salesman must try to persuade his customers to attend. If it is not possible to produce at least one compelling reason why every customer should visit the exhibition, then there must be serious doubts as to the value of the company participating at all. If an exhibition is not attractive to buyers, then it does not serve its purpose.

7 *Films or filmstrips*

Within the last few years a number of film-producing companies have succeeded in developing a market for promotional films. These films are useful for showing the processing of certain manufactured goods such as steel, and in particular those that must come from overseas. The films may then be shown at collective meetings for dealers, distributors, customers and even students. They have been found particularly useful in the computer industry, where complex instructions need to be conveyed accurately to operators, programmers, systems analysts, etc.

The Trade Descriptions Act

In addition to its voluntary Code, the advertising industry is subject to a great deal of legislation, including the Trade Descriptions Act. Other legislation that affects advertising administration includes the Merchandise Marks Acts 1887–1953; the Sale of Goods Act 1893; the Misrepresentation Act

1967; the Food and Drugs Act 1955; the Trade Marks Act 1938; and the Sale of Goods (Implied Terms) Act 1973.

The Trade Descriptions Act, which came into force on 20 November 1968, lays down new codes of commercial conduct and was passed to give greater protection to buyers by strengthening the existing law against false or misleading descriptions used by sellers of goods and services.

Under Section 4 of the Act a trade description is defined in the following way:

(a) When it is used 'in any manner likely to be taken as referring to the goods', and it therefore includes any advertising or sales promotional material.

(b) If goods are ordered against a description and are supplied against that description, then the supplier is deemed to have applied that description to the goods.

(c) Any description added to the goods themselves or to any document with which, or any package or container in which, the goods are supplied.

However, the law does recognise that certain claims which amount to an expression of pride and are not statements of fact cannot reasonably be classed as misleading, although such expressions as 'best on the market' are now being used less and less by advertisers for fear of prosecution under the Act.

Section 5 of the Act deals specifically with advertisements and extends liability to the information contained within advertisements. In the case of prosecution, the advertiser, its agency and the media-owner are all considered liable. However, a medium is believed to have a good defence if it can show that the advertisement was received for publication in the normal way of business, that it was accepted in good faith and that there was no reason to suspect that its publication would amount to an offence.

What, in fact, the Act amounts to is the likely prosecution of any trader making a false or exaggerated claim of any kind, or even a claim that is true but misleading when referring to goods he sells or offers for sale. However, prosecution in practice will only follow if the claim is considered false or misleading to a material degree.

The advertising industry lays down its own strict codes of conduct. The Advertising Association and the Institute of Practioners of Advertising in conjunction with the media-owners operate the Code of Advertising Practice. The Independent Broadcasting Authority has used this Code as the basis for its own code, which incorporates the requirements of the Television Acts and the Broadcasting Act. Few anti-social campaigns get by these invigilating bodies. The industry fully recognises the need for control of its powers by those who understand them.

The practice of public relations

The practice of public relations goes far beyond the recognised business of press relations, exhibitions and seminars. Public relations are concerned with the development of company recognition due to its forthright policies and its frank and practical manner in dealing with the people within its environment. No matter how successful a company may be in dealing with and gaining support from the communications world, its public image will in the end depend on its true business attitude. Based on the modern proverb that 'actions speak louder than words', the company that enjoys sound public relations has made a conscious effort to build business relationships upon mutual trust and respect.

Many companies do not have a specialist public relations department. Yet their deeds will spread among those that have some vested interest in the firm's existence, whether they be suppliers or customers. This approach to a company's image, although modest and praiseworthy, is also regarded as passive. The modern attitude to business development requires an active effort to promote company achievements. In a world where many companies are flooding the communications media with newsworthy items, few reporters have the time to search out and record the performance of the modest.

All firms, no matter their size or number of employees, have a public image, ranging from the impressions gained from visiting salesmen to the view casual passers-by get of the premises. Images are created by actions as diverse as telephone-answering manners to road usage by identifiable company vehicles. Opinions of a company may be formed by visitors who have to avoid water and soap-suds on the shop floor or by friends and relations of past and present employees. It is in this area of public attitude that so many companies suffer from a poor public image, not simply because they ignore the opportunities available from the need of the media to fill their columns with interesting news and developments.

Public relations is often regarded by other business functions as the sweet that is handed out when medicine has to be taken. This can never be so. Good public relations have to be earned in the same way that a lasting marriage has to be earned. In an age where management techniques, attitudes and terminology are subject to constant innovation and change, it is difficult to keep the entire population abreast of individual company actions and their causation.

Although public relations and advertising use the same media (or at least the press relations part of public relations does, along with press and television advertising) they are in no way directly comparable activities and do not compete as business functions in any way. The two activities should be considered complementary as they both aim to achieve the same objective, but in very different ways. Public relations depends upon a statement of facts, creating a climate of good-will by enhancing sales opportunities, expressions of company policy or objectives in order to ease recruitment or the raising of finance. It is an activity devoted to securing the co-operation of employees, customers, suppliers, shareholders, and potential employees and their families. It differs from advertising because its editorial or broadcasting coverage is not paid for, and therefore the information must rely on its newsworthy content in order to be given coverage by the media. The job of PR is to make news releases newsworthy.

Advertising, on the other hand, makes claims; it aims at direct sales. The material is of such potential importance to the advertiser that, in order to have it presented exactly the way he needs, he is prepared to pay for its appearance. As they appear in the advertisement columns these claims are clearly recognisable as claims made by the manufacturer for his own benefit, no matter how factual they may be.

So editorial coverage is probably the result of a continual PR campaign which has created sufficient interest for an editor to want to give all the facts to his readers. This achievement is rarely free, for the company concerned has had to devote resources to the PR function.

It is considered unwise to try to evaluate editorial coverage according to costs of advertisement space because:

(a) Editorial coverage is an expression of facts and therefore does not contain the same persuasive element that is characteristic of advertising.

(b) Editorial coverage carries more weight because it is considered to be more objective since it is what other people say about you, whereas advertising is quite clearly what you say about yourself.

(c) Editorial coverage is always subject to the availability of space and many, to the advertiser, valid points may be edited out and a balanced view (i.e. that most favourable to the advertiser) lost.

(d) Editorial coverage is not pre-tested for customer acceptability and it is possible that an unfortunate choice of word or expression may cause considerable damage, even with an otherwise favourable review.

However, without such explanations in terms meaningful

to the population, company actions may be misunderstood and harmful interpretations placed upon company policy. A company that has fostered public awareness will have helped to build a 'confidence' bank, so that when the unexpected happens, such as a strike, public opinion may be favourable and more disposed to believe the announcements made by the management than those by other sources.

While most non-marketing executives are acquainted with the idea of public relations, few are acclimatised to the idea that the sole aim of a sound public relations policy is the creation of goodwill. Goodwill is regarded as being the value of the business, i.e. the price it could expect to bring on the market, less the realisable cost of assets such as land, plant and machinery. It is the premium that some other firm or individual is prepared to pay for the company as a going concern rather than as a stockpile of assets.

At one time a product or a business generated its own goodwill. But that was when goods available on the market were limited even for the well-to-do. Even then it would have been difficult for one firm to promote its image, for in the day of unbranded goods the reputation of the manufacturer was entirely in the hands of the retailer. At that time the retailer had almost the power of life or death over a firm. And this is still true today, despite the demise of so many corner shops, because the supermarket has assumed considerable power through the strength of its purse strings and through 'own-label' products. So while there was a gap for some thirty years or more in which the shop or store took a back seat—the days of the sellers' market—it is distribution that accounts for success in the consumer goods industry. It is often the esteem in which a firm is held, the image it has or has cultivated, that is the decisive factor. A persistent public relations policy should pay real dividends.

This is also true of industrial goods companies. Being reported favourably in the popular press, and having certain of its technical skills featured in the trade press, may often bring substantial benefits to the company. As with the service industries, where advertising is either forbidden or even uneconomic, suitable press commentary is an aid to the promotion of the facilities provided.

But where public relations really does make a difference is in differentiating one product from another. So the organisation that is able to instil confidence in the purchaser has the edge over the unknown firm. For the buyer is, in fact, purchasing the corporate 'personality' of the organisation inherent or embodied within the products it makes or supplies.

It is therefore vital to a company that everyone with whom it has dealings, whether they be shareholders, suppliers, employees, customers or the influential 'City', is favourable towards the company and its policies. No better example of good public relations is available than that of Marks & Spencers, with 'customer satisfaction guaranteed' and sound employee relations, or of Sainsburys with its 'value for money' reputation. The image of these companies has spread partly because of realistic management policies and partly because of the mediocre approach of so many of their competitors. But it has spread mainly because of the extensive distribution networks of the two organisations, which ensure that both companies' names and their policies become 'household' property. Normally a company has to employ a definite policy of promoting public relations, so building a 'confidence bank' among its markets by dispensing news currency at frequent intervals.

Two-way information flow

It is usually insufficient for a company merely to send out 'puffs' to the press, radio and television. It is necessary to obtain some feedback of the impact of company policies. To send out information and not to obtain public reaction is as valueless an exercise as reading a book and not understanding the words. So, in addition to informing the public about the organisation, the public relations function must present to the management of the firm an accurate, objective and balanced interpretation of public attitudes.

To do this the public relations practitioner develops an intelligence network and service which will attract input of all aspects of public opinion and attitudes. Moreover, to make his efforts fruitful, he provides for his clients the method and the means by which the current state of the environment in society's thinking may be tempered to suit both his clients' needs and his clients' customers' needs. Simply to tap the resources without directing them to the mutual benefit of both supplier and consumer is clearly not in the long-term best interests of manufacturers.

It follows from this observation that public relations as an activity is a direct reflection of the client it serves. A company that adopts lavish expenditure on public relations instead of pursuing sound commercial practices is doomed to failure even more quickly than might otherwise be so. For example, nothing incenses a customer more than seeing replicas of his unsatisfactory purchase praised, without foundation, in some trade journal. In response to a complaint the journal will soon redress the balance. The faulty practice will soon get its just deserts. The two-way flow of information is therefore beneficial to all deserving parties.

8 Publicity—II

Sales promotion may be distinguished from advertising not only in actual practice but also in matters of emphasis. The major objective of all advertising effort is to persuade people of the advantages of ownership and of the profits its use will bring. Sales promotion is devoted to inciting people to buy, and to buy now. So sales promotion supplements the process of advertising by reminding people, often at the critical decision-making stage, of the benefits of an immediate purchase. Sales promotional activities therefore often take the form of an incentive, a short-term buying advantage.

Sales promotion is often identified as the activities 'below-the-line' in publicity, the 'line' being an undefined arbitrary division of expenditure on press advertising—the 'demand pull'—and on sales promotion—the 'sales push'. Furthermore, it is because the line is ill-defined that dispute arises as to the true meaning of each term used—necessarily, because so many forms of publicity are in their infancy and, in reaching for maturity, the different activities tend to be interchangeable and dependent upon the influences of the firms that offer the services. They are in a constant state of flux. Hard definitions are soon challenged and found to be wanting.

Sales promotional methods

As sales promotion campaigns tend to be short-lived they are, almost by definition, used to solve short-term problems which are, nevertheless, ever-present. A sales campaign in a particular region, either related to a chosen product or aimed at a specific class of customer, is the ideal marketing problem for sales promotional activity. So although any one sales promotion idea is short-lived, it fits into the overall marketing programmes as a short-term solution to a never-ending problem—sales performance and growth.

Sales promotion is often divided into three key areas:

1 Consumer promotions
2 Consumer pricing promotions
3 Permanent promotions

Consumer promotions and consumer pricing promotions both follow strictly the short-term emphasis of promotional activity, while permanent promotions quite clearly do not. Some further consideration of all three areas is advisable.

1 Consumer promotions

Although consumer promotions are often surprisingly effective in particular campaigns, they do tend to be the subject of a considerable backlash. Often one finds that a successful promotion precedes the product concerned being left off the shelves altogether. This may well suit those companies able to switch production facilities at short notice, or those that have found overstocking at some point in the distribution network and need to force goods through and build demand. It is not such a useful device for a company needing to boost its sales effort and hoping to win a long-term market share by such methods.

The normal consumer promotions are:

(*a*) Sampling—house to house with coupon
(*b*) Sampling—in-store plus coupon
(*c*) Coupons—through the door
(*d*) Coupons—through selected media
(*e*) Premium promotions (the daffodil)
(*f*) Bonus pack (extra portion)

(*g*)   Money-off
(*h*)   Self-liquidating offers

These techniques are often known as incentive marketing and have been a growth industry since the advent of television advertising, coupled with self-service, helped them to take off. They are all the result of volume sales—or, to be more precise, anticipated volume sales.

Sampling is without doubt the best method of launching a new product, but because of the often considerable expense involved few firms are prepared to risk the investment it demands. Yet, assuming the product to be good, sampling does allow trial and appreciation at each distribution level, since people are often glad of the opportunity to try a product before spending money. Sampling also has the advantage of exercising some influence over those people who would not normally experiment with new products. Sampling proves to be most effective when prospects are selected in advance and the approval, through sampling, of distributors is won, and particularly when some form of in-store demonstration runs concurrently with the sampling period. The most critical aspect of using samples is to ensure that the sample is an exact replica in pack and form of the product to be put on sale.

The provision of coupons is a price concession and at best no more than a substitute for sampling. As is usual in the business world, the usefulness of coupons declines in proportion to the amount of money spent on them.

Consumer promotions do, however, have a part to play in marketing tactics. Experience has shown the methods are best suited to:

(*a*)   New products with a distinguishable product advantage
(*b*)   Products in competitive growth
(*c*)   Supplementary promotions

They are least effective:

(a) For established products, particularly if sales are declining
(b) When unsupported with other brand promotions.
(c) In an aura of constant pricing promotions.
(d) As a defensive measure in intense promotional competition

These conclusions are drawn from the conclusions and experiences of numerous promotional executives. Yet each of these executives is able to relate a case history where the conclusions were different from those stated above. This indicates that, as a general rule, the above conclusions are correct, but the inspired marketing man may well defy them and succeed. And that is true of any 'rule' of marketing management.

2   Consumer pricing promotions

Tactical pricing promotions tend to be the promotional method most often encountered, probably because it is the easiest to choose and often the simplest to justify. But it is frequently based on the often fallacious argument of high-volume low profit margins. Pricing promotions are best undertaken from positions of strength. Rarely do they work when things are going badly. If sales are growing and a pioneer or market leader wishes to expand the total market and/or to, win market share from a smaller competitor, then a pricing promotion can be very effective—but only for a short period of time. If continued for too long, the promotion will backlash on the manufacturer.

Sometimes an advertiser wishing to achieve wider distribution may embark on a pricing promotion while maintaining trade channel margins. This assists distribution, but only where the outlets anticipate increased sales. That often means the full support of an extensive promotional campaign.

The rules on tactical pricing are quite clear:

(a) Consumers identify a price with value for money. They

often resent prices returning to normal after an extensive campaign. They may switch to a competitive brand whose price has been maintained.

(b) The flow of supply and demand often works when price promotional activity takes place.

(c) Price promotions are most beneficial when offered as two packs for the price of one or, as suggested earlier, through couponing. Making a straight reduction often incites the consumer to stock up while the special offer is running. There are, in addition, a number of variations on consumer promotions and pricing, and these may often produce impetus to sales, particularly if the theme is being pioneered.

3 Permanent promotions

Such promotions are often critical to the success of certain product lines. Where demonstrations are essential to a purchase, such as with cars, then a permanent showroom has to be maintained. Just like promotions in supermarkets, showrooms need to follow certain rules. For example, a sports car or a convertible may attract a customer into the area, but because of family needs he will probably buy a saloon. However, he may never have entered the showroom if it were not for the sports car in the window.

Often, for instance in garden centres, the consumer is best attracted when he sees a product in its natural setting. This is why so many products on sale in stores have illustrated examples showing just what the buyer is capable of producing.

Clearly there are some products of which it is impossible for the salesman to carry samples or even for the typical store to make a display. Boats are an example. Yet boatsellers are canny; they try to avoid being too close to water, because otherwise selling becomes a matter of frequent demonstration and infrequent orders.

The mobile exhibition has become a feature of current promotional activity and offers cost benefits for companies where permanent exhibitions are essential to the main selling effort.

A technique now being used successfully by some companies is the permanent showroom in a department store or a retail chain shop. The company concerned hires space within the premises and takes advantage of the traffic flow of the store to provide sales opportunities. A number of travel agents are operating in this way, as are some suppliers of soft furnishings. For some years a number of cosmetic manufacturers have signed franchise agreements within such a framework.

Merchandising

Conclusive purchasing decisions are made at the point of sale, now increasingly referred to as the point of purchase. The part of sales promotion that provides the final impetus, reassures the prospect and makes it easy for him to buy has become known as merchandising. Among its practitioners it is known variously as the 'silent salesman' or as 'selling through' techniques.

It owes its present position in marketing to the advent of self-service. The depersonalisation of retail selling necessitated an alternative to the sales assistant—a system that performed the functions of the seller but without the costs involved. The system, in other words, had to sell. And because of competition at retail level the function of selling itself had become more critical.

Failure to put the product in the right place and at the right time frequently means no sale. Because the fight for shelf space grows more intense, the need for sales per square foot is critical. So the manufacturer must ensure that his sales performance matches the terms demanded by the retailer. The manufacturer, in fact, must now provide the means by which his product sells at the point of purchase. He has provided advertising. He has used sales promotion. And he must merchandise. To achieve this aim he uses specially trained salesmen, known as merchandisers, who are skilled in product display, store layout, and promotional techniques and production. Merchandisers are now commonly used in grocery, hardware and chemist's shops.

It is therefore clear that merchandising is the means by which a manufacturer and his retailer combine their resources in the common aim to increase sales. Obviously the other forms of publicity are an aid to the retailer, and in the case of coupons he actually assists the manufacturer in a promotion. But this is co-operation. Merchandising requires the guidance and promotional materials of the manufacturer—based on his selling strategy—and the facilities of the retailer. Yet the aims and goals of the two are different. The retailer's needs are:

1 To bring prospects into the shop.
2 To increase store traffic (the circulation within the shop).
3 To sell a full range of products.
4 To maintain shop loyalty.
5 To increase average spending.

It is clear from this that the retail outlet has little interest in individual products but is mainly concerned with maximising its asset, which is a *point of purchase*. So the retailer wants fast-moving goods with healthy profit margins. Sometimes the retailer will require help in announcing a new line or in selling off slow-moving goods. These are often the subject of a special offer. The needs of the manufacturer, however, are:

1 To ensure that distribution reaches the shelves.
2 To obtain a prominent selling position.
3 To provide product recognition.
4 To provide shopper identification with the product.

The manufacturer cannot achieve these objectives by using merchandising alone, for the technique is but an integral part of the marketing process. Without the full support of the marketing programme, merchandising may well be wasted.

Merchandising depends for its success on the discernible behaviour of the consumer. Although research findings are limited, some commonly accepted criteria have emerged. For example:

(a) The prime selling spots are gondola ends, eye-level shelves and the checkout area. Children are vulnerable to confectionery carefully placed within their reach, and if the unit value is low mother will pay.

(b) Shopping habits involve twenty minutes in a familiar supermarket and no shopping lists with the majority, although a clear idea of purchases needed is usual. The average shopper knows the location of pre-selected purchases and removal of particular goods is semi-automatic.

(c) Decision-making is rarely a matter of conscious thought at the point of purchase. If not predetermined, then it becomes an irrational purchase, often through self-indulgence.

The activity of merchandising involves the layout of a store, the deployment of display material and the reflection of house style. But it is in the combination of these methods that merchandising is most effective. They need to be considered in some detail.

The layout of a store
It is the merchandiser's aim to provide a traffic flow situation in the shop that encourages a steady progression through the entire store but where each diversion carries an incentive to continue around the store. The store wants maximum exposure of its range to the highest possible number of shoppers. Often the slow-moving, less popular lines will be placed in prominent positions, for the fast-moving commodities will usually be searched for by brand-loyal shoppers. As consumers appear to shop in a daze, it is common practice to place dump bins in the centre of traffic lanes, so ensuring full attention as the house-

wife walks round them. Some merchandisers have to act as supervisors to shelf-fillers, many of whom are local housewives earning pin-money.

The deployment of display material

All stores receive more display material than they can usefully use. Competition for the limited space available for showcards, shelf-talkers, display cases, mobiles, swing tickets, headboards and many others is tough. So the material must not only *be* capable of moving products but must also *appear* capable of moving them. Frequently the decision as to what is to be used comes as a directive to the store from head office. It may often be the result of a central purchasing agreement. Increasingly the super stores and the voluntary chains are producing their own display material.

The reflection of house style

Certain retail chains have recognised the merchandising advantages of house style. Often house style is a direct reflection of the retailer's own marketing strategy. It is this development which has led to retailers providing their own display material. This is obtained to show the appropriate image for the store consistent with its need to attract the consumers it has chosen to serve. Promoting a house style is usual in other forms of publicity where collective impact exceeds what would probably have been achieved with separate advertisements. The house style promotion has developed with and parallel to the 'own label' package. In this case the retailer puts his own reputation at stake in branding a manufacturer's line with his own name.

So although expenditure on below-the-line publicity declined somewhat in 1971 and 1972, the merchandising of goods remains as pressing a problem to the manufacturers as ever before. But because of the consistent wastage over many years, manufacturers have been attempting to improve the quality of their merchandising systems and hence the absolute volume has declined, though higher prices are being paid for improvement in quality. There is still much scope, however, for merchandising in non-food lines.

Packaging

Packaging has been an essential feature of the trading scene since man carried water or milk for sale. Today in the UK some 2% of the gross national product is spent on packaging materials. In the early days packaging was primarily used for security of the contents. In the case of gunpowder or corrosive materials, security was also needed for those who actually handled the goods.

But security is no longer the sole requirement, for packaging may incorporate considerable selling power and may often be used to establish identity, to provide information on its contents and their use, to suggest the care needed in handling and, significantly, to supplement the merchandising effort at the point of purchase. Packaging is therefore capable of being used as a powerful promotional medium. It is, in fact, increasingly becoming a full-bodied marketing communications channel.

Part of the progression from bulk packaging to unit packaging is attributable to the widespread adoption of branding. At the same time many local producers became uneconomic and production units were increasingly devoted to a few areas of a country, with output being distributed through fast-developing distribution networks. So the physical handling of goods over long distances, the exposure to the elements and the sheer time needed in transit created real needs for better packaging.

Modern packaging facilities mushroomed however, with the arrival of commercial television and the adoption of self-service trading. As in merchandising, the package assumed a vital role in the selling of the product at the point of purchase. Furthermore, because the product would be demonstrated on television—in its pack so that it could easily be identified—the need for superior packaging became clear, and with colour television now on the scene the need is intensified.

Today's consumer, it is said, lives in an era of abundance. To the psychologist many of the tensions of modern life are associated with the problems of choice. Present-day neurosis is often attributable, it seems, to the almost infinite variety of choices facing the shopper. To the manufacturer, however, it suggests the need for a positive approach to making it easy for the purchaser to buy. By providing easy recognition, clear benefits and an attraction in the packaging itself, the manufacturer exploits his opportunity, but in doing so he fulfils a felt need. In addition, the package can provide a unique promotional opportunity, for the advertising message on the pack may be seen after the purchase in the home every time the product is used. When stored, say, in the kitchen, its pack is a constant reminder to the housewife. Even when the pack is empty it provides a promotional activity—because it needs replacing.

Packaging as a marketing tool

Packaging is a critical part of the marketing mix and frequently appears as marketing strategy. If the product for sale is usually bought as a gift for someone else's consumption, then more money spent on the container than on the contents may be desirable. For example, some brands of cosmetics tend to sell on 'their appearance on the dressing table' rather than on their appearance on the face or body. Similarly, cutlery sets customarily bought as wedding presents may be more appealing to the purchaser if the package infers an expensive gift. There are numerous variations on these strategic themes.

1 A new pack may provide an uncountered promotion.
2 A new pack may revitalise flagging sales.
3 A new pack may extend the product life cycle.
4 A new pack may revitalise the 'trade' interest.
5 Seasonal variations may be avoided by deep-freezing.

6   Packs may be designed for ease of handling.
7   Packs may be designed for economy in transit.
8   Costs may be reduced through packaging technology.
9   New markets may be entered through packaging technology.
10   Established markets may be reborn through packaging technology.

The major innovations in packaging in recent years seem to be in the use of plastic film, aerosol, frozen foods, dehydrated foods and prepared foods. The emphasis is as much on convenience as it is on the actual package, so a complete new service strategy has evolved from packaging principles. But packaging as a strategic weapon is not the complete story. The design of a package may be deliberately aimed at reducing pilferage, shop-lifting being a major problem in all classes of outlet. It also has a prime function to perform in ensuring the safety of the contents. Efforts must be made to prevent access of rodents if food is stored for any length of time, as should the migration of inks and glue be prevented. Equally important is the avoidance of loss through destruction or deterioration of the contents.

Packaging as a behavioural tool
In this era of mass production real product differences have almost disappeared. Packaging is a means by which the consumer is able to distinguish one product from another, either because it adds an extra service element or because it provides some psychological satisfaction. In a society that has enough to eat, adequate clothing and shelter, and almost all the material things of life, it is often the satisfaction of deep-rooted desires such as social acceptance, feelings of superiority, and freedom from fear and danger that give a product the edge it needs over competition. So packaging may give a product its unique selling proposition. In that sense, the package becomes indistinguishable from the product. 'Dimple' whisky, potato

crisps, hairsprays and long-playing records are examples of products for which the package seems almost indispensable. Clearly there are some products where this is completely true, such as photographic film or medicines, but these are security measures rather than added value.

Colour is one of the most useful ploys in conveying psychological ideas about products. Perhaps it is a direct reflection of developed dress-sense or even a natural association taken from habitual usage. For example, white is known to convey impressions of cleanliness and purity. It is emphasised in detergents, it is the colour of the traditional wedding dress and it has long been a feature of hospitals, both in decor and in medical staff dress. Other colours and their associations are:

Black   — strong, overpowering
Blue   — cool, distinction
Brown   — utility, general
Gold   — royal, rich
Green   — natural, quiet
Orange — warmth, mobility
Purple — lush, extravagant
Red   — hot, excitement
Yellow — warm, sunshine

Different shades of these colours may accentuate or soften the idea to be conveyed. For added emphasis a combination of colours may be used. Orange and black is frequently considered a highly sensuous combination, while green together with the two blues of Oxford and Cambridge (the colours used for the European Marketing Congress) convey modesty, coupled with intelligence and dynamism. So in the shopping centre, associations of ideas may create favourable or unfavourable buying habits. Colour can therefore be used to sell.

Direct mail

Although scorned by many, direct mail is probably the most

versatile of all the advertising media, for it is the only medium that is capable of being matched with the individual requirements of any or of all advertisers. It can be directed economically at a few or effectively at many. The advertisement may be sophisticated or simple, as required by the advertiser. He is not obliged to use the accepted inflexible format usual in other media.

The two most constant criticisms of the technique are that there is a high wastage factor and that mailing lists soon become outdated. Each point is true. But these weaknesses are recognised, and can be measured and minimised. If the required success ratio for a mailing is 5% and a mailing list compiled over five years has a known success ratio of only 1%, then investigation of the mailing list will reveal different success ratios for each year of the five-year period. If the two most recent years have an average ratio of 10%, then it would be worth while undertaking a mailing to the addresses acquired during that period. No other form of advertising can combine selectivity and objectivity in this way.

Direct mail is so versatile that it can be used as a market research tool. Although it has some limitations when compared with telephone or field research, it does enable the researcher to operate more economically and it provides more opportunities for the informant to consider questions without haste and, where necessary, to obtain supporting information.

As a marketing tool the technique has much to commend it. For apart from this market research potential, the medium makes customer profile compilation possible and the end product realistic. These profiles may then be subjected to considerable analysis and should provide an investigator with the basic data essential to the development of a formula helpful in calculating a propensity to purchase.

The profits will also prove useful in winning customer confidence. Because direct mail is, or at least should be, entirely personal it is possible for the advertiser to take advantage of the information contained within his profiles by emphasising some private detail or characteristic, so suggesting to the prospect a highly personal offer.

The benefits of direct mail

The benefits of direct mail are contained within its differences when compared with other media. These basic differences are:

1 It is selective
2 It is confidential
3 It is non-competitive
4 It has flexibility
5 It has originality
6 It has no schedule
7 It can be modulated
8 It can be timed
9 It can include action aids
10 It provides feedback

This is an impressive list of attributes considering the limited appreciation for the medium. But of course these benefits are not automatic, they come as a result of careful and considered use of the facilities available. Some detailed consideration of these benefits is therefore warranted.

1 It is selective. A direct mail shot may be sent to particular individuals or to groups of individuals in one market precisely, and therefore more economically than other media, and in particular to small or unusual sectors. There are firms that specialise in compiling such lists and often they will offer a guarantee as to the accuracy of their lists.

2 It is confidential. Only direct mail achieves complete confidentiality—if necessary. Because each mailing shot is addressed to a particular individual and may be sealed against alien eyes, it can convey messages of privacy or even those of an intimate nature.

3 It is non-competitive. Advertising has to battle with competing claims for attention. Commercial breaks on television may be used as natural breaks, while newspapers need a 60:40 ratio in favour of advertising to survive. Outdoor and transport advertising, posters and signs compete against the counter attractions of the real living world. But direct mail arriving in the post has the maximum possible chance of winning attention—it may even monopolise the breakfast table.

4 It has flexibility. Apart from postal regulations and the restrictions imposed by common sense and good taste, there is almost no limit to the size, shape or format for a direct mail shot. Similarly, there is extensive scope for the use of materials and productive processes.

5 It has originality. Because of the considerable flexibility in the styling of a direct mail shot, it is possible to incorporate a creative element in the advertising used, almost to the point of complete originality. Certainly there is scope for initiative or inspiration. This is particularly significant in a world of near homogeneity of available products.

6 It has no schedule. Unlike newspapers, magazines or television, where timing of publication or broadcast is essential, direct mail letters may be sent out at the convenience of the advertiser. Admittedly he is restricted to some extent by the work programme of his production department or of the mailing agency.

7 It can be modulated. Big things from small beginnings could almost be the motto for any mailing campaign. The advertiser may run his campaign regionally, using the returns from one area to subsidise his action in the next. He could divide the total market into product groups, or market segments, and build up business by tackling one part at a time.

8   It can be timed. Because direct mailing has no schedule other than that required by arrangement between the advertiser and the mailing house, it is possible for mailings to be made to suit any event or occasion. So launching a new product or giving support to a major campaign can be programmed as needed.

9   It can include action aids. Reply-paid postcards or order forms can be included, making it easier for the prospect to take action. Most marketing men are concerned with overcoming apathy and so any aid to solving that problem is welcomed.

10   It can provide measurement. Because the mailing list is preselected and the advertisement developed specially for that market, it is possible for the advertiser to monitor his results and so establish a rate of returns. In this way he is able to identify the profit performance of his advertising.

Direct mail shows every sign of becoming the medium of the future. Like the selling faction, it needs only to establish a respectable image. Moreover, it is typical of our society that direct mail appears acceptable to the professions whereas all other forms of advertising are not. Perhaps when direct mail becomes respectable it will be avoided by dentists, estate agents, accountants and so on. For even they cannot ignore the fact that it is soliciting for business.

9 Selling and the Sales Force

Selling is the most dynamic force of marketing because it is the only activity that generates revenue—the life blood of a business organisation. It may be true that certain other activities are revenue-raising, such as advertising in a mail order operation, but invariably they are but a substitute for selling effort. Consider an advertisement in a newspaper inviting business through the post: it is an impersonal selling action. It is, in fact, using those parts of the selling operation that may be presented graphically. The other aspects of the selling process come later when the customer either approves or returns the goods delivered.

Selling has always been a part of trading, and trading has a history as long as civilisation. It was selling that made the division of labour possible, long before Adam Smith wrote about his pin-maker. But during the early days of trading, selling was preoccupied with satisfying existing demand by locating and identifying prospects and convincing them of the items' merits as compared, perhaps, with alternative purchasing opportunities. Today selling is equally involved with the development of a latent need into a positive demand.

The change in emphasis happened at the time of the Industrial Revolution. Historically, traders had their wares made in the cottage industry, similar to that prevailing today on the Isle of Lewis for the production of Harris Tweed. The turn to machines in the nineteenth century meant centralisation of production. It also meant a considerable increase in productivity. Previously, merchants had traded in local markets, while the more enterprising sent the surplus to the neighbouring big city. This was on a modest scale. Then suddenly with machines churning out unheard of quantities, albeit at a low unit cost, it was essential for the merchant to tackle entirely new markets. Moreover, because of the volume involved, he was unable to perform the necessary selling function alone. So he hired salesmen to sell—to sell to people who had little knowledge of the utility of the products concerned. Now with the help of the salesman they had to be persuaded to change their attitudes and 'invest' in a better living. The cumulative effect was a phenomenal growth in demand, in production and in the standard of living. Therefore the stimulus for creating today's wealth among the industrially advanced nations has been a result of the selling process.

The art of communication

The practice of marketing is described in this book as common sense and the ability to communicate. Because common sense is comparatively rare and, like all human characteristics, is unequally divided between the personal faculties, pursuits and attitudes of the individual, true selling ability is uncommon. Besides which the problems of communication are such that they are probably responsible for the greater part of dissension between peoples throughout history. Yet the salesman was the original marketing package. All other marketing activities have evolved to supplement and, hopefully, complement his performance. So the practice of marketing and the benefits it brings to society originated in the salesman. In fact, the truly professional salesman has practised marketing doctrines for as long as the history of trading.

The salesman sets out to persuade. He persuades by concentrating on the satisfaction, or the prospect of satisfaction, of deep-rooted desires. The salesman is aware that people purchase benefits—what a product does for them—not just the product for its own sake. Often consumers are able to relate this logically in their own minds, for when a person buys a spade it is because he wants to dig a hole in the ground or needs to move something from one spot to another. A spade is the means by which he satisfies his need. It happens sometimes that the buyer is only partially aware of the purpose behind his or her purchase. Buying an expensive pen will allow the purchaser to write only marginally better, graphically, than he would with a cheap pen, but the pride of ownership, much of which may be latent, may be a positive reason for the extra cost. There are other occasions when the person has no real idea of why he or she has made a purchase. Buying a new hat which may never be worn is, possibly, a means of relieving 'pent-up' emotion. Many impulse purchases in supermarkets —selling through the silent salesman—originate, it is believed, because of self-indulgence, itself generated by boredom or by a desire to reject any form of discipline irrespective of whether it is self-imposed or otherwise. Salesmen learn to recognise the signals that the customer gives out, in much the same way that we in our social lives recognise the symptoms of boredom, anxiety, anger, frustration or excitement. It comes from a constant study of people.

Before we consider the fundamental desires inherent in the human personality it is necessary to see how the salesman uses his own knowledge of physical attributes to communicate. Basically, people communicate in two ways: knowingly and unknowingly. The professional salesman uses both. He uses the techniques of planned selling to communicate knowingly and the five, or perhaps six, senses to communicate 'unknowingly'. Let us consider unknowing communication first.

People judge others by what they experience on contact with them. They use their senses to do this:

1 Sight
2 Sound
3 Touch

4 Taste
5 Smell

The salesman takes great care to provide better than acceptable standards in the normal sense. He will also continue to use his understanding of these 'sense judgements' to communicate. By the use of these senses he communicates enthusiasm, sincerity, drive, interest, understanding, earnestness, consideration, integrity, knowledge and industriousness. The list is not exhaustive. Study of the classified columns of The *Daily Telegraph* will produce a never-ending list of essential selling characteristics. In selling it is not enough to be merely good, it is necessary, modestly of course, to show it. And it wins the confidence of customers and produces orders.

Nevertheless, the wise salesman does not stop at personal communication of this sort. In addition, he provides sales aids to reinforce his own personality and to provide further communication opportunities.

Exploiting innate desires

Selling people what they really need is not only a marketing philosophy but also a psychological appeal to their deep-rooted desires. Psychologists compare the human personality to the iceberg. Man allows but a part of his total personality to be revealed, leaving the greater portion beneath the surface, hidden from all but those closest to him. So he remains unmoved by the surface winds, no matter how strongly they blow. He will, however, tend to move with deep ocean currents as they play against his great bulk below the surface. For example, a person may not notice abuse from an opponent but may be deeply upset if reminded, say, by his children that his voice is unworthy of the latest hit record. Every one has the basic desires this example supports. The actual blend is unique to the individual, but no one is totally without a portion of each. The fundamental desires are:

1 Food and drink
2 Comfort and shelter
3 Freedom from fear and danger
4 Social approval
5 Self-esteem
6 To attract the opposite sex
7 To love and be loved
8 To live longer

This list encompasses all the sources of human emotion. Often these emotions may show in some physiological form, such as sweating, a dry mouth, goosepimples, tears or as tension shown in backache or neckache, toothache or headache, and so on. But the more pleasing aspects come from that part of the personality which makes people likeable. These are positive factors which, although often exploited by sellers, nevertheless bring great benefit and satisfaction to the people concerned.

1 Food and drink
Few people in the advanced countries today really know the effects of hunger or thirst and so their satisfaction has ceased to be recognised as a basic drive. But the experiences of the few driven to cannibalism and the like under extreme conditions are surely an indication of what could be. Besides, it was only a hundred or so years ago that children of 8 or 9 years old risked being hanged for stealing a loaf of bread.

2 Comfort and shelter
Once again, the experience of total withdrawal in limited to few, but the many thousands anxious to buy their own homes in the face of prohibitive prices must experience some emotional upheaval, enough to drive them almost to distraction.

3 Freedom from fear and danger
To twentieth-century man, the motor car, smoking, alcohol

and over-eating provide the real dangers. Fortunately, the incidence of danger appears so remote that the average person does not believe its consequences could happen to him. Certainly a direct confrontation with the possibilities of danger usually proves to be anti-productive. Posters on road accidents, and safety-belt and anti-smoking campaigns appear to have been ignored by the majority.

4 Social approval

Many successful marketing campaigns have prospered through customers wishing 'to keep up with the Jones'. The part of built-in obsolescence that promotes the annual face-lift or change of model is a direct appeal to this human need. Caravans and boats are items that seem to owe much of their saleability to the prestige ownership seems to bring.

5 Self-esteem

Each person must have self-respect. To do so they must experience a feeling of superiority. To be able to respect themselves everyone must believe they are a little bit better than the next man, and that whatever they do is always the result of better thinking or judgment. Everyone thinks this way, and everyone needs to think this way. It is why so many advertisers feature their products in a setting totally untypical of the average purchaser. The average purchaser tends to visualise himself or herself in that setting. Often, of course, they do not *see* the quite considerable differences. People establish a close affinity with the environment of their daydreams—an association of roles and circumstances.

6 To attract the opposite sex

Freud expressed this desire more blatantly, but prudence has changed the basic drive to that of the chase rather than the kill. However, in selling or advertising terms, the principle is a continuing best-seller. Even if Freud was wrong, and that is disputed, in describing it as the strongest desire, in modern marketing terms he could not be more right.

7 To love and to be loved

The theme has been used for a detergent, for frozen peas, tobacco and numerous other products. It appeals largely to the maternal instinct and to young love. The makers of Persil have persevered, and one assumes succeeded, with their theme of maternal love and 'whiteness shows'. Oxo's Katy has been a universal winner in projecting family love and togetherness. Others are less certain.

8 To live longer

Judging by the amount spent on health there is no shortage of scope for the seller, provided that it can be substantiated. There are some 'services' that cannot.

These eight desires demand satisfaction. In the past, religion was almost the only solace for the working population. Even today the only real hope of satisfying all these desires seems to lie in self-discipline generated by religious faith. Yet the most rewarding aspects of these desires seem to be the positive ones. Freedom from fear and danger, and the desire to live longer are comparatively weak areas for the salesman to work on. The insurance or assurance salesman must never state the obvious, but if he speaks in positive terms, such as tax benefits, savings potential, security of income and the like, he seems to gain good results. Salesmen win orders by satisfying such needs.

It is by showing the prospect that his real, unspoken needs may be satisfied that many successful salesmen make use of the 'sixth' sense. Not many people admit to understanding how it works, for it is often known as a female intuition. In the selling game it involves providing psychological clues which win the unwitting approval of the customer, so establishing an almost telepathic relationship. It is because of this contrived personality trait that good salesmen are described as 'born salesmen'. In fact, it is more likely that successful salesmen tend to come from the highly perceptive members of the community: those that feel mood and sense attitude, and respond accordingly. By so reacting to need they sell themselves to prospects. And when they have won the genuine confidence of another person, then that person rewards them accordingly.

Clearly people who succeed in selling could just as likely have succeeded in the theatre, in politics or as social workers.

Organisation for selling

Now that the mystique of selling has been dispelled, let us consider a more mundane and yet, for the vast majority, a more critical aspect—the organisation of the selling job. In any case, the personality traits already specified are within everyone, for we all practise the principles described in order to mix well and to live our everyday lives. The better salesmen tend to be particularly perceptive, but that is a talent which can be developed with training. However, no salesman succeeds who does not organise himself in his selling job. To be successful he practises the principles of planned selling. This means having a plan of campaign for each customer, knowing exactly what products it will profit the customer to buy and the benefits the salesman can emphasise that will encourage him to buy. Arranged carefully, this approach will enable the salesman to increase the number of orders he will collect. The sales presentation he will have worked out will flow quite naturally once the method is understood. For it enables the salesman to direct and control an interview, knowing at all times the route he is taking through the buyer's mind. Planned selling consists of:

1 Building business
2 Journey planning
3 The sales sequence
4 Personal organisation

Each of these activities is essential to successful selling. As they are the vital means by which the salesman makes his contribution to the firm's prosperity, it is advisable to consider each activity in some detail. Although they will be considered separately, it must be understood that they are interdependent.

1 Building business

The commercial and industrial scene is constantly changing. Firms close down and others start up. Some move away and others move in. A few will change buyers, some favourable and others unfavourable to any one concern. A small proportion will be growing rapidly and a few others will be declining. In a period of five years the total market situation is likely to have changed beyond recognition. So the active salesman will not only be ensuring that lost business is replaced but will also be continually finding and winning new customers.

To build business a few definite disciplines must be followed. First, the salesman must reserve a portion of each working week to the business of opening new accounts. While the better part of this time will be devoted to obtaining relevant information, it should include a fixed amount of time spent with prospects. In addition to providing opportunities for bringing in new business, it will also assist the salesman in maintaining his presentation at a high pitch, for habitual calling on established contacts allows bad practices to develop.

Often the best business building prospects are contained within a salesman's established customers. A number will buy a limited amount of supplies from a range of suppliers, giving the bulk to one or two trusted firms. The active salesman will prepare for each prospect a detailed specification of needs and buying habits. He wins the confidence of buyers by showing an understanding of their problems and by offering suggestions and ideas. Because of his travels and because of the information fed to him by his employer, he is able to become a focal point of industrial information. By coupling his knowledge and by using his own firm's resources, the salesman is soon able to become the major and the most reliable source of information to buyers. Now, while this does not mean that the buyer will automatically reward the salesman by showering him with orders, it does ensure that the salesman is always seen and this alone increases his face-to-face selling time. He must use that valuable time effectively. The professional salesman sets himself targets for such activity performances.

2 Journey planning

Time is the most valuable commodity of the salesman. He must use it wisely. Sensible buyers appreciate the value of a salesman's time and do not allow it to be wasted. Buyers that place restrictions on time devoted to seeing salesmen are simply not doing their job. Good commercial buyers believe that their most fruitful activity is listening to salesmen. They believe that salesmen bring profit opportunity. Sadly such buyers are rare. In some countries they are almost non-existent. In the UK they appear to be company secretaries, office managers or even clerks whose minor function is to see salesmen, collect literature for filing and to make occasional complaints. These people totally disregard the buying function, except at Christmas when they expect to collect their turkey or some such reward. The buying decision in these circumstances may not be in the best interests of the employers. The practice is certainly not in the best interests of the national economy.

The salesman attempts to maximise his selling time by planning his daily journey. This may be aided by gluing a street guide onto hardboard, sticking in coloured map pins to indicate calls and then putting elastic bands—of different colours—around the appropriate daily journey. Through preselecting a particular route the salesman learns to economise on time by estimating his arrival at each call and he is therefore able to fix appointments for a number of calls, particularly those at the beginning and the end of the day. Furthermore, he is able to allocate the amount of time he spends with each prospect. Now he is in a position to devote his best time to the best prospects.

As he works out his daily calling programme the salesman sees the advantages in travelling during non-selling time or while buying propensity is at a low peak. He makes his longest journey before the start of the working day so as to arrive at his first call promptly. Any necessary travel during the day will be between the hours 12.00 and 2.00 p.m. This enables him to maximise his face-to-face selling time. Alternatively, that time may be spent in the local library catching up on current events in the locality and, in the reference section, up-dating customer profiles.

Ideally, the salesman should use a time-planning analysis record, showing a breakdown of the major activities of each day totalled into 'selling time' and 'non-selling time'. By keeping this analysis he is able to carry out improvements in his daily work programme. Besides, the salesman should regard himself as a production machine, with a schedule prepared to furnish orders.

3 *The sales sequence*

The sales sequence is often confused with a standardised sales presentation. The standardised presentation is a prepared sales talk developed by experienced salesmen. While it has the disadvantage of sounding stilted and artificial when put into the mouths of unknowing new recruits, it does give them a vocabulary and provides them with early confidence in their selling job. Properly understood it will also give the basis for a sound yet flexible presentation after induction and following some applied experience.

The sales sequence is based on the same principles but is developed by the salesman himself with the aid of his field sales manager. In effect it is a work programme for the selling activity based on the capacity of the individual and the needs of his employer. The sales sequence is the essential implementation of the company sales policy. In recent years it has become incorporated in the company sales manual. It is based on:

   (*a*)   Company sales policy
   (*b*)   Attitudes to the buyer
   (*c*)   Company products and services
   (*d*)   Securing interviews
   (*e*)   The sales talk
   (*f*)   The presentation
   (*g*)   Closing the sale
   (*h*)   Overcoming objections

In order to understand how the salesman undertakes his selling job it is beneficial to consider the details of the sales sequence more thoroughly.

(*a*) *Company sales policy.* The sales policy is usually contained within the marketing plan and may often be revealed through study of the sales budget. Investigation will reveal the quotas set for the numerous activities of selling, apart from achievement of sales performance in the chosen product mix. Salesmen that simply pursue increased sales turnover are not necessarily choosing the most profitable route. In some firms a £500 order may bring infinitely more profit than a £5000 order, even though relative profit margins, say 10%, are the same.

(*b*) *Attitudes to the buyer.* The buyer is not a machine, he is a human being. He trusts people he likes and distrusts those he doesn't like. He makes the best and most rational decision that is possible. But the larger part of any buying decision is one of judgment and so it is emotive. He will pay more for one of two identical products if he believes it to be more reliable, or that the maker will ensure that it is trouble-free. He is prepared to pay extra for freedom from doubt. Like every other buyer, he suffers from cognitive dissonance and he tries to avoid it by paying a premium price. Even if the merits of two competing companies are unknown to the purchaser, he may be prepared to pay more, believing that he is getting better value for money. Moreover, because the prospect is human, he likes to be considered knowledgeable. It is not unusual for the salesman, knowing a new product is about to be launched, to discuss with buyers the needs for a new product, carefully noting the advice of each prospect. If he guides the interview along the right lines he gets at least three constructive suggestions from each buyer, knowing that they are already incorporated in the new product. When the product is launched he visits each prospect in turn, thanking them, on behalf of the company, for their valuable help and showing them the product they have helped to design in accordance with their own expressed needs. Where possible he follows this visit up with a letter of appreciation so that the buyer proudly shows it round. That letter must include details of the specific points made by the buyer. By showing it around the buyer is 'selling' the advantages to his colleagues.

One word of advice. This technique must not be overdone. Furthermore, stressed points made by the buyer and not incorporated in the product must be treated as buying objections and resolved accordingly.

Too often people think that salesmen have to be good talkers. It is true that they have to persuade, but persuasion is best carried out by the individual on himself. Buyers are no exception. So the salesman is essentially a good listener. By asking the right questions he gets the buyer to make his own buying pressure and to overcome his own objections. In doing this he ensures that the interview is devoted entirely to the interests of the buyer—and also, as it happens, to the long-term interests of the seller. It gives the buyer the feeling of importance he needs—a feeling common to all buyers. It is why they seek the job.

(*c*) *Company products and services*. As we have seen, successful marketing depends on satisfying the real needs of the buyer. The buyer does not buy a machine, he buys profit, output or opportunity. He must be sold these benefits. So knowing one's product is not as important as knowing what it will do and what it will not do. Likewise, the seller shows that he knows how his product compares with competitive opportunities.

Furthermore, the salesman studies his company's supporting services. He knows when to offer credit, how the tax system benefits a purchase now, and how maintenance and service contracts, where appropriate, operate. The buyer must never be allowed to find supporting information for himself. The successful salesman has supporting aids in the form of dcf calculations, feature articles from the quality press, a prepared list of questions and answers, reports on the usage by approving customers and a specially written specification suited to the prospect. In his covering letter the salesman refers to particular points raised by the buyer and indicates where explanations may be found. He makes sure that the buyer is given better than full acknowledgment in writing for the part he has played. The professional salesman gets his reward and satisfaction in the form of orders, not by trying to prove to the buyer what a superior salesman he is. Good salesmen never sell, they find buyers shrewd enough to buy from them.

(d) *Securing interviews*. In general, more calls mean more selling time. And that means more orders. Now this does not mean that the salesman must devote himself to maximising his call rate at the expense of all other considerations. It means that he should conduct an interview with an objective in mind, secure that objective and depart. More time spent in preparing for a call results in less wasted time during the call. This is the first step in ensuring an interview. The salesman with an objective in mind has a worthwhile reason for calling. It is not merely another contact visit. The buyer soon learns that his caller is always worth seeing—he will always get something of value from him.

Once in the presence of the buyer it is essential to win his instant attention. If the salesman fails to win the buyer's interest within the first twenty seconds, his success barometer falls drastically. So he gives the buyer something to do. The buyer is given something to hold—something to look at or feel, to taste or smell. He is not talked at because his mind is still full of his immediately previous activity. That spell must be broken. In the absence of all other inspiration, a copy of the local paper thrust into his hand followed by a question on the lead item will often do.

The objective at the interview must never be to secure an order. Salesmen make customers. The objective is to satisfy the buyer's need with a product beneficial to him. The interview must be devoted to that objective, and prepared and undertaken accordingly. The opening remarks always refer directly to the problems associated with the need. By high-lighting the need the buyer is attuned to the direction of the interview. He is made to realise that the salesman understands his problems and is willing to be a helpful ally in their solution. All human characteristics prevail in the animal kingdom. Often points of human failings or strengths are illustrated by reference to a particular animal. Now we have much to learn from dogs. Dogs are man's best friend because they will always greet him with enthusiasm and excitement. A tail may even seem to be wagging the whole body. Taking a hint, the salesman will always try to show his delight at seeing the buyer. He may do this with the warmth of his greeting or he may use the magic of a smile—few people feel that they can resist a smile given freely and without inhibition. Smiles make a person look more presentable and they engender friendliness in the meeting.

Each interview is therefore the preparation for the next. Securing the first interview may be difficult, but with a definite objective and something relevant to say an approach by letter or telephone can prepare the ground. When suggesting an appointment the salesman gives the buyer two alternatives to choose from, by time and by day. He does not leave him with the choice he may adopt himself—a yes or a no.

(e) *The sales talk.* All sales points need to be credible. The seller contrives to provide supporting evidence. He uses his voice as a persuasive instrument: variations in tone and pace, liberal uses of pauses, supported by the hands for explanation —either by gesture or by writing down a point for the buyer to see as well as hear—are all necessary. The use of words is important. The salesman chooses active verbs—at least 50% of all verb forms used should be active. Moreover, half of all nouns used should be concrete. Adjectives and adverbs should only be used when they are needed for precision. Where they are used to express opinion, then that is made quite clear to the prospect otherwise there are dangers arising under the Trades Descriptions Act. Prepositions are always to be preferred to prepositional phrases. Meanwhile, the salesman who succeeds takes great care to perfect his diction and English usage. Often he will rehearse his presentation on tape and amend the unsuitable—and he may even rehearse in front of a mirror so that he can vet the image he is projecting.

(f) *The sales presentation.* These are the golden minutes of selling. It is where all the preparation counts. The major selling points appealing to the motives of the particular buyer are supported by visual aids or by a demonstration. At each step the seller tries to get the agreement of the buyer to the point being made. At the finish of the presentation the salesman repeats the selling points that appeared to attract the prospect the most. All the time looking for buying signals, he probes for the real, perhaps hidden, reason behind the more active interest shown by the buyer.

(g) *Closing the sale.* Because they fear rejection, many people fail as salesmen, simply because they will not ask for the order. The best salesmen try to judge the point at which the opportunity for agreement is best and then suggest some alternatives for the buyer to choose. They do not give him the chance to say yes or no; rather they suggest black or white, 100 or 200, delivered next week or next month.

Thus the seller encourages the buyer to make a choice between one of two favourable alternatives.

(*h*)   *Overcoming objections*. Properly prepared, the sales presentation will overcome objections before they arise. But some strategy is necessary. Buyers like to buy. They do not like being sold. Now if the salesman presents a faultless case, the buyer will create an objection so that he can be seen to be performing his buying job. He also needs some time to grasp the essentials and he will find this time by raising an objection with no real foundation. In other words, he will raise objections that cannot be overcome because they are purely fictitious. We all do this. We see something we like, but we have to consider every alternative before returning and deciding on the preferred purchase. Experienced salesmen know this characteristic and leave minor faults in their presentation so that the buyer can spot them and feel he is doing his job. Because they are minor faults and because they are deliberate, they may easily be overcome. Honour is satisfied.

4   Personal organisation

Organisation can be the essence of good selling. The personal organisation of the salesman, who is away from an office, a secretary and a convenient telephone for much of the time, is critical. Apart from planning his time he must constantly be analysing the market and finding prospects. He must keep adequate records of customers, their transactions and dealings, and their potential, together with relevant industrial information. Furthermore, he must write informative sales reports such that the content is as valuable to him as it is to his management.

Successful selling is one of the most rewarding careers open to man. It provides him with untold opportunities. But the greatest danger to beware of is being recognised as a 'good' salesman. If he looks like a salesman, sounds like a salesman and behaves like a salesman, he will fail because he cannot be a salesman.

10 Selling and Sales Management

Selling has been shown as the most dynamic element in the business environment. Yet despite the disciplines inherent in the planned selling method, salesmen need directions. It is not that they, as a breed, are unable to decide their own priorities but that each sales territory is only one part of a larger and wider selling operation. Although the individual salesman may well be competent to judge the changing market situation locally, it is unlikely that he will have the time and the skills necessary to *anticipate* these changes. Furthermore, whatever the local situation and its changing demand scales, the salesman must sell the product mix most profitable to his company. So although he, in isolation, may find that he is able to sell a different mix more easily, he must either adjust his activities to meet company needs or advise management of the possibilities on his territory. From this advice the company may find it expedient to substitute some parts of his quota with those of a salesman in another territory with a similar problem. In this way one may compensate for another. By co-ordinating the activities of the members of the sales force in this way, the sales manager performs one of his most critical operational tasks.

The job of sales manager is analysing the market, recommending selling strategy and then recruiting the sales force needed to achieve pre-set sales goals. He is responsible for control of the selling effort.

Before considering the job of the sales manager in some detail, it may be advisable to relate the sales manager's position to that of the marketing manager. Essentially, the present-day job of the sales manager is no different from that which he has always practised. But there was a transitional period during the emergence of mass advertising, market research and information management when the sales manager's role changed. He became responsible for these support-to-selling activities and became the marketing manager. Because of the changing emphasis it was thought in some circles that the role of the salesman was finished. Management attempted to substitute the salesman role, easily the most expensive market communication activity with supporting activities. But it soon recognised that the salesman was still the most effective seller of goods and services, even if the most expensive. Once this was recognised, sales managers were appointed to make the best possible use of this costly asset. The job of sales management, then, is the deployment of this asset in the most profitable manner.

In some companies the marketing manager reports to the sales director. This apparent anomaly arose in companies where the sales manager's job remained pre-eminent but where marketing services, including publicity, research and planning, had been put in the hands of a newly appointed marketing manager. In these companies there was never any doubt about the value of the salesman.

The job of sales management

For convenience the sales manager's job may be divided into the following categories:

1 Planning
2 Organisation
3 Recruitment and selection
4 Training
5 Running sales meetings
6 Motivating
7 Directing

8   Monitoring
9   Harmonising
10 Field sales supervision

It is clear from this list that the real job of the sales leader is management. Man management is the central theme of any sales leader's task. Historically, skills in management were considered a natural in-born talent, a flair which somehow coincided with intelligence. This view has now been largely discarded. Knowledge of management is acquired in much the same way as knowledge of engineering or accounting. The relationship between knowledge and ability is not, however, so close as it is in the natural sciences. Despite their own considerable knowledge of management techniques, people still fail. Moreover, people without such knowledge sometimes succeed. What does seem clear is that there is a better chance of success with knowledge than there could be without it. The sales manager is no different from any other functional manager; he needs to practise skills developed from a realistic body of knowledge built up over many years by men of experience. The sales manager uses this acquired knowledge to perform his job.

1   Planning the selling effort

The first priority of the sales manager is in the planning of his own time. He must first establish his priorities, allocate time to the various tasks, develop a workable schedule and delegate the minor functions he cannot handle personally. By following this procedure he stands some chance of fulfilling his programme. In sales management all crises seem to arise at the same time and all targets likewise come into sight together. If time is not rationed and priorities predetermined, the sales manager could easily sink beneath the flood of calls on his time.

But this policy will work only if his overall planning procedures are within his capability to control. The elements within his span of influence are:

(*a*)   The salesmen
(*b*)   The sales territories
(*c*)   The customers
(*d*)   The products

As the emphasis here is on planning, it is the future trends that matter, and these are subject to the continuing influence of the sales manager. His plans for each of these performance determinants need separate consideration.

(*a*)   *The salesmen*

Salesmen have always been judged by performance. They grew up with payment by results, principally because of commission on sales schemes. Although the measure of performance principle has not changed much, salesmen today enjoy a measure of security through combined salaries and incentives.

It is perfectly equitable to measure salesmen by their performance, one against the other, provided that their opportunities are equal. In actual practice, however, they do not enjoy such equal opportunities. Unfortunately, it is almost impossible for the individual company to measure market sales potential in sufficient detail and with the necessary accuracy. It is also impractical to constantly change territorial boundaries because potential has changed. So management needs some other means of comparing and measuring *selling* performance as opposed to *sales* performance. The most appropriate method is to decide the activities necessary to perform the selling job, to apply weighting factors and then to establish quotas accordingly. These activities include the number of calls, selling costs/enquiries, cost per call, average value of orders, canvassing calls, number of orders obtained, etc. (See the author's book *How to prepare a Marketing Plan*.) By establishing clear programmes of activities for salesmen and by working out conversion ratios for every activity, the sales manager is providing the basis for his future selling efforts. He is therefore planning the activities of the salesman.

(b) The sales territories

It has already been said that calculating market sales potential by territory is really beyond the scope of the ordinary small-to-medium firm. Notwithstanding this point, it is still necessary for the company to estimate at least the present market size, the company share, and industry and company growth prospects alike. But even this data is unlikely to be as helpful as a sales analysis showing company achievement on each territory preferably by product, by size, by class of outlet and, where possible, by direct marketing costs. Moreover, information as to gross profit earned by territory and the number of dormant accounts when compared with the national average should indicate the likely areas of attack. These will then be included in the plan of campaign devised to support the field salesman.

Where possible, each sales territory is built up from distinct regions for which separate statistics are available. These may be by county, by Registrar-General's regions or by television areas. By conforming to these boundaries it is possible for a company to make use of published statistics in planning for growth. In the absence of other factual information it is possible to calculate national averages per head of population and to use these figures as a determinant for market size. Provided that the sales manager realises that the figures he is using are no more than indicative, he may find them significant in planning terms. For example, if sales penetration on a territory is far beneath the national average, then reasons may be sought. Investigation often reveals a clue to improved sales. In practice sales managers may allocate sales territories according to number of outlets. Although useful, it does not allow for growth potential, nor for really significant amounts justifying additional attention.

(c) The customers

As we have already shown, customers' operating performances do not always move in a uniform pattern. Their suppliers, in their own interests, need to identify the growth opportunities confronting customers and then to concentrate their energies on supplying those that seize these opportunities. To grow is to serve growth markets.

Sometimes a company may have to select customers with the necessary potential and then guide them towards opportunities. Whichever applies, the companies concerned must be selected from among the many. Some will be very small, others may be large. Between the two extremes will be concerns capable of buying a successful small competitor and so improving their own potential. Sales management is the function that controls the activities necessary to bring orders today and reports to top management on the opportunities *in the market place* tomorrow.

To carry out this analysis all customers and potential customers are grouped according to size by SIC (Standard Industrial Classification). Changes between groups are soon spotted and causes investigated. Furthermore, where a company has a diverse product range it will subdivide the analysis into product groups. This may appear a mammoth task, but it is probably already extracted in those companies most likely to adopt the system in its preparation of the sales forecast. In really large companies it is no more than a print-out from the computer, while small companies, on the other hand, will not have so many accounts to investigate.

Marketing-orientated companies are those that consider the implications on customers of every critical business decision. So monitoring the performance of these customers is just as necessary a part of the marketing frame as it is an essential control device for sales management. Besides which, the information needed by sales management on customers will be contained within the customer profile records kept by the salesmen in order to perform their everyday selling task. Such

is the desirable structure of marketing information systems—
entirely modular in nature.

(d) The products

The sales manager influences product policy and product
development, because he alone is able to advise on the continuing conflict between volume and price from purely market
conditions. He may not have the skills to equate supply and
demand quantitatively, but because of his communicating role
between customer and management he is able to provide the
necessary qualitative appraisal. This subjective approach is
critical because sales returns do not arrive by discrete units as
shown on a demand curve, they arrive by customer order.
Moreover, orders are not of equal value, nor do they have a
'normal distribution' among customers. Price increases hit the
biggest buyers hardest. They also find it easy to secure alternative sources. And they will, if their assessment of service
supplied shows a negative differential to the likely price difference. Mathematics will not identify this possibility—the
sales manager should. The price elasticity of demand remains
his province. In this position he provides guidance on product
policy decisions and tends to represent the interests of his
customers when such discussions take place. Planning the
selling effort is an essential part of the marketing plan. The
benefits of the effort are derived from the disciplines involved
in producing the plan, looking for answers and preparing
solutions.

2 Organisation of the selling effort

The sales organisation is created and maintained in order to
achieve the company's 'rolling' objectives. There is no one best
type of sales organisation and the different types each have
their merits. The choice of a particular organisation will have
depended partly upon the circumstances facing the company
and largely on the resources available.

Sales organisations have gone through some change during

the post World War II period. Clearly this transition has been parallel to the changes in the patterns of distribution. Selling to a new distribution channel demands a different selling organisation. Often the change is made in order to ensure control over the firm's actual selling effort, rather than leaving it to a distributor of some kind. Avon established its own network of sales girls in order to short-circuit the restrictions inherent in the franchise system prevailing in the cosmetic industry. Tupperware brought its party-plan selling ideas to the UK and was quickly matched by Sarah Coventry and Pippa-dee. Pyramid selling won many early recruits but quickly became discredited. Other changes in the organisation of selling effort involved the use of revitalised promotional devices and aids, and the reduction of personal sales contribution; mail order, vending machines and self-service are prime examples. These changes were prompted by the costs of sales personnel, the need for superior and more leisurely presentation, and the advent of volume sales. They are more easily subjected to a routine selling procedure, with less versatility required at the point of purchase.

However, four considerations are essential in the organisation of a sales force:

(*a*)   The need to serve the customer
(*b*)   The duties and procedures involved in serving the customer
(*c*)   The personalities required to serve the customer
(*d*)   The degree of responsibility and authority necessary to make decisions regarding the customer

All decisions affecting the sales organisation must be taken in full consideration of the present and ultimate effect upon the customer. The choice between agents or distributors as an alternative to salesmen will be taken according to the needs imposed on the manufacturer by his customers, for the sales organisation is provided to serve the customer and is an essential part of the 'added value' he expects in the price he pays. The actual types of selling organisation prevailing conform to these criteria. Each type involves a different *degree* of selling, combined with a required supporting qualification. In practice many firms recruit a technically qualified man in the belief that he will sell better because he is technically compatible with both the customer and the products. The argument of this being a better alternative to the experienced salesman being taught sufficient technical knowledge is invalid. Both succeed as well as fail.

These selling jobs are:

(*a*) Speciality selling
(*b*) Pioneer (or commando) selling
(*c*) Industrial selling
(*d*) Consumer durables selling
(*e*) Consultant engineers
(*f*) Missionary (or propaganda) selling
(*g*) Repeat consumer selling.
(*h*) Retail selling
(*i*) Merchandising

Not all these need amplification. Speciality selling is practised generally where there is a once-only selling opportunity, or at least where there is little likelihood of a repeat sale in the near future. It is a selling job which requires the salesman to assess a need and sell his line all at the same interview, usually from cold. Reward is largely by commission, and because of the pressures involved turnover of personnel is high. The system includes assurance salesmen, some office equipment salesmen and those selling advertising space, although this category is fast moving away from the speciality field, the exception being in the sale of some directories and annuals.

Missionary or propaganda selling is almost unique to pharmaceutical products. Salesmen call and 'sell' to doctors who do not buy but specify to chemists who do not consume but supply to patients who have no choice. Other selling jobs are easily identifiable to the non-marketing executive. What is common to them all, however, is the tendency to reject the salesmanship aspect of the job by emphasising the 'representative' expression. This is but a sop to the salesmen: everyone knows what his job is—it is he and his management who try to pretend it is something different. This may be for good reasons, but it is still unnecessary.

3 Recruitment and selection

The sales manager of today has considerable help in recruitment. He may have a personnel department or he may use a selection consultant. If he does the job himself, he has the *Daily Telegraph* and he has *Selling Today*, the journal of the UK Commercial Travellers Association. Recruitment presents few horrors to the sales manager, unless it be the sheer volume of applications he is bound to receive. Selection, however, is the real problem. As no one has resolved the problem of what makes salesmen succeed and, if they do, why they cannot repeat their performance in another company or another industry, the sales manager's task is unenviable. He must use his judgment. Provided that he has analysed the selling job adequately and prepared a realistic job description, and then used this in conjunction with merit-rating reports of his best men to produce a man profile—a description of the type of man most likely to succeed in the job—he has improved his chances of success immensely. But no more than that.

Some of the most commonly specified characteristics are:

(a)   To be perceptive of people's attitudes and needs
(b)   To have ambition, motivation and be a self-starter
(c)   To indicate presentation, health and poise
(d)   To show business sense, curiosity and mental abilities
(e)   To suggest courtesy, friendliness and persuasiveness
(f)   To generate creativeness, knowledge and originality
(g)   To provide enthusiasm, flexibility and integrity
(h)   To have figure sense and good handwriting and speech
(i)   To imply loyalty and self-control

A man who has all these talents would not necessarily make a good salesman, but they are typical, in part, of the most desirable characteristics. In the selection process it is not unusual for the salesman to be put in the hot seat. It is a position he will occupy often enough when confronted by customers.

4 Training the salesman

Salesmen spend most of their time without direct supervision. They are continuously going through the same routine, numerous times each day, of presenting their products, and emphasising and re-emphasising the benefits of particular products. In return, they hear every day all the reasons why most prospects do not buy from their company. Some of the remarks may be derogatory, others may simply state why their existing suppliers are superior. Under such constant pressure it is not surprising that an individual salesman becomes disorientated. Training is intended to provide a satisfactory balance to the problem. Furthermore, during the course of his journeys the salesman is constantly mixing with the salesmen of other companies and industries. He will tend to adopt the general characteristics of these people unless his employer takes the trouble to give him training in attitudes, work habits and procedures. Salesmen are good at their jobs because of their chameleon-like personalities, changing to every mood and responding to every whim of the customer. If they are not given regular training and reorientation they soon become biased in favour of their customers.

The better form of training will usually consist of a combination of theoretical instruction and practice in the classroom and practical training on the job. Training for new recruits or retraining for established salesmen will normally consist of:

    (a) *Background knowledge:* the company, its history and

organisation; procedures and routines; policy; long-term plans; promotion policies. The industry, formation, structure, market shares, competition.

(b) *Work planning and organisation:* journey cycles, selective selling, customer records, information seeking, prospecting for business.

(c) *Sales techniques:* customer needs, preparation of material, obtaining interviews, sales presentation, sound talking techniques, overcoming objections, closing, selling after-sales service.

(d) *Supporting the selling effort:* product knowledge, reporting procedures, administration, entertaining, merchandising, personal promotion, car driving.

By providing a training programme the sales manager is obliged to analyse the selling job and to develop standards of performance. This makes it possible for the salesman himself to spot his own deficiencies and remedy them before they become apparent to his colleagues. Eventually a training programme will bring sufficient discipline and guidance to help avoid major deficiencies arising at all.

5 Sales meetings

The sales meeting is used as a vital training activity. The more preparation the sales manager puts into the meeting, the greater the results. In establishing his sales meetings' programme through the year, he starts off with a clear objective and makes sure that the reason behind each meeting is clearly defined. Consistent with clear-cut objectives is the adoption of a theme for each meeting, each theme conforming to some part of marketing strategy. Having adopted real commercial reasons for running the sales meetings, the sales manager uses some form of monitoring device to enable him to seek and find improvements.

Meetings are beneficial to the salesmen and the company

alike because they help to consolidate the link between management and the sales force. This often eases the stress on communications. By providing a forum the sales manager gives an opportunity to those within the company to mix and discuss common problems. Moreover, the gathering together of the men fosters a sense of belonging and reminds them of the vital contribution each makes to the company's well-being. In addition, the sales meeting is the ideal occasion to explain new policies, company plans, projects and developments, and the members of the sales force are able to contribute and exchange information about new ideas, notable achievements and sales tactics. In this way the sales manager reinforces his training programme. The alternative themes open to the sales manager may include:

(a) Achieving the forecasted product mix
(b) Opening and developing new markets
(c) Prospecting for new business
(d) Using sales promotional material
(e) Record-keeping
(f) Selling the after-sales service
(g) Converting inquiries to orders
(h) Selling expense cost ratios

These are no more than indicative of the range of subjects the sales manager may use. Ideally, the year's programme will be built up from an analysis of selling problems recorded in the annual marketing plan.

The sales meeting is the platform upon which the sales manager gains or enhances the respect of the members of his team. Even well-known public speakers have some trepidation before speaking. This may show at the start. However, once into his subject, the sales manager should soon interest his men in what he has to say, for he should be close enough to them to speak their language. To ensure that he makes the most effective impact he attempts to:

    (a)   Highlight the most relevant points
    (b)   Emphasise the importance of the subject
    (c)   Use visual aids
    (d)   Start with a practical example
    (e)   Make his own enthusiasm contagious

Because he realises he is making a sales presentation to his men he adopts the techniques involved in a proper buyer/seller interview. He ensures that every step follows a logical sequence and is qualified by examples and illustrations sufficient to register with the audience. He uses pauses to let points sink in. He does not use too much detail, for that may be contained in handouts, and instead concentrates on making principles clear, for they are most likely to be remembered. And to reinforce his presentation he summarises his major points, so shaping the talk as a whole in the minds of his listeners.

6   Motivating

There are two kinds of motivation: financial and non-financial incentives. Because of the unique nature of their employment salesmen are particularly sensitive to both types of incentive. They know that a little extra effort on their part may bring huge rewards to their company. So by having a payment-by-results scheme the company encourages it salesmen to greater effort by allowing them to share in the benefits they bring. So although money may not be the most important motivator, it is certainly the most powerful and may often be a substitute for the really important incentive. For like his customers, the salesman is subject to the iceberg principle and needs satisfaction for all his eight basic desires.

Yet financial incentives do work for many men and in others they may act as a substitute for satisfaction of real needs. Salesmen operating on salary only tend to recognise the value of the technical support service they provide and get on well with their customers; sometimes it is often difficult to determine exactly where their loyalties lie—with the customer or with their employer. The major advantage from the employer's view is that the salaried salesman is more easy to control than a commissioned man. Commission-only salesmen work solely for financial reward. They tend to concentrate on getting orders and often minimise attention to supporting services since, for them, they take up valuable selling time. Because they are paid on commission alone they may easily work for more than one employer and so devote their time to the more lucrative areas of their territory, making no real attempt to develop their patch.

The salaried man is a cost to the employer irrespective of sales revenue, while the commission-only man is paid out of revenue and bears the risk of the enterprise. Most firms today attempt to compromise between the two extremes and provide a combination of salary and commission; where commission is not easy to evaluate because of a team selling effort, a bonus to salary is provided.

The typical salesman, however, reacts positively to some form of non-financial incentives, simply because the nature of his job makes him seek solace of a more emotional kind. Normally these non-financial incentives consist of:

(a)   Recognition and appreciation
(b)   A feeling of belonging
(c)   A personal challenge
(d)   Good working conditions
(e)   Leadership
(f)   Security

Although these are all straightforward, each one has special connotations for the salesman.

(a)   Recognition and appreciation

The job of selling is a simulation for the winning of approval. Salesmen are continually struggling to satisfy their need for acceptance. Much of this need can be satisfied by the process of winning orders. However, in the selling job today, once sold a new customer will often place orders direct as goods are required. This robs the salesman of his regular 'shot'. So a form of compensation is provided by the sales manager during the time he spends with salesmen in the field.

(b) A feeling of belonging
Because of the time spent away from home, with many lonely nights spent in hotel bedrooms, and the isolation away from his colleagues, the salesman may develop lone wolf symptoms. This is dangerous. Selling demands a gregarious animal, so the sales manager attempts to provide a 'feeling of belonging' to the sales force. He often does this by sending them information, by asking their advice and through news letters keeping them in touch.

(c) A personal challenge
Setting targets or quotas gives a man something to aim at. By giving him goals the sales manager is removing uncertainty and inviting co-operation.

(d) Good working conditions
To the salesman this means a respectable car, reasonable travel and accommodation expenses, and a system of working that he can easily follow.

(e) Leadership
Everyone needs to feel that there is someone to whom they can turn in times of stress: someone in whom they have confidence and who is capable of inspiring them to greater effort when circumstances warrant it.

(f) Security
It is a fallacy that good salesmen reject security. What they do reject is the limitations to immediate reward that come with secure jobs. Salesmen usually come from a breed that equates

reward with effort, and in order to enjoy the opportunities this may bring they are prepared to accept some of the risks. Salesmen do not differ from any other person in the need for security. But they are more willing to absorb some of the wider variations in their fortunes, to rely more on their own skills rather than sink them into a general pool, and to take their chances accordingly. Their need for security shows in their efforts to succeed.

7 Directing the sales effort

In Chapter 9 the need for a time-planning analysis for salesmen was stressed. Earlier in this chapter it was shown that the sales manager needs to plan his time effectively. The emphasis on time is not unrealistic. Out of a 365-day year the salesman averages 250 working days after weekends and holidays have been deducted. If he makes his first call at 8.30 a.m. and his last at about 5.30 p.m. he has managed an 8-hour day, of which about two-thirds may have been spent in travelling, parking and waiting to see the buyer. He needs to be kept waiting only an average of 10 minutes per call for as few as six calls a day to have wasted an hour. Parking may take a similar amount of time. So the salesman has a productivity problem. He needs to maximise his time. The sales manager in helping his men to overcome time problems by, say, saving each man one hour per day, will have increased their total available time by $12\frac{1}{2}\%$ and their actual selling time by a staggering 40% to 50% .

Similarly, salesmen do not always recognise the value of their time. Study of records often reveals that a salesman will call six times a year on accounts placing orders twice a year with values between £5 and £50. Working out the cost of a salesman's selling time at, say, 3 hours a day 250 days a year equals 750 available selling hours. Taking the cost of the salesman on the road plus his car at £4000 per year, we can see that his selling time costs £5.30 per hour. There is clearly no profit in such calls, particularly when one considers that the supporting services behind the salesman, all linked directly to his returns, may cost as much again or more than his own direct selling costs. The sales manager shows him how to make the most effective use of his selling time. He helps him to divide his accounts into categories, showing the vital calls, the desirable calls and the low-priority calls. From these he is expected to select the best 100 prospects—100 because normally a salesman will be unable adequately to serve more unless his job entails little selling and much straightforward order-taking. There are, of course, extremes: a computer salesman may work on six prospects while the milkman will serve 400 or more.

To help his men become more productive the sales manager sets quotas for their activities as well as their performance, and:

(a) Helps them to prepare their journey plans
(b) Guides them on calling times
(c) Encourages them to make prior appointments
(d) Shows them how to prepare presentations
(e) Co-operates with selective selling
(f) Urges them to ask for an order at any call

8   Monitoring the sales effort

This exercise is best performed in the form of a merit-rating guide. This should be completed in the presence of the salesman, making him understand the reasoning behind every observation recorded. It is essential that the salesman understands that the system is used solely for his benefit. When introducing such a system it has proved prudent to let the salesman retain the merit-rating sheet and then ask him to produce it subsequently at a later date for comparison. A merit-rating form may contain:

(a) Personal qualities
(b) Job knowledge

(c) Personal organisation
(d) Salesmanship

The qualities detailed under each headings are normally contained in the job specification and the related man profile.

At the same time the sales manager is compiling his own records on his salesmen. This form of measurement will be an evaluation of each salesman's activities and how he performs against the national average, most of this information being obtained from daily report of call sheets. At least once a month the sales manager will write to a salesman drawing his attention to some point on the call sheet. He would do this even if he has had no time to study all those submitted. Salesmen conclude that all are being studied.

9 Harmonising the sales effort

Sales territories do not divide nicely into convenient segments. Some substantial users buy through the head office in London. Who gets the credit? It is the sales manager's job to ensure that such happenings are equitably resolved.

10 Field sales supervision

Field sales supervisors have been used in recent years to carry out that part of the sales manager's job that he finds most time-consuming yet is most vital in the performance of his job, even if his management colleagues do occasionally feel that a reply to their memo about the carpet in a branch office is more important.

Field sales managers are used to bring about sales expansion. As we have already seen, the salesmen's selling time is critical. It is the job of the field sales manager to make that selling time truly productive. He does this by implementing, in detail, the policies outlined in this and the previous chapter. He takes responsibility for planning, training, leading, motivating, directing and controlling the selling effort. He helps the salesmen to create customers, and customer satisfaction and good-will.

The function of sales manager may well be undertaken by the chairman of a company if the customer is significant. Consider the story written by W. J. C. Geffers, Fellow of the Institute of Marketing:

'In the 1930's when Lord Hurst first became Lord Hurst and was Chairman of the General Electric Company he was responsible for the business which was done with the Grey-hound Racing Association and in fact we were their only electrical suppliers. I was asked by Lord Hurst's secretary to make an appointment for him to see Lord Loch and was to get several alternative dates for them to lunch together. This I arranged and a convenient day was fixed and I was then told that Lord Hurst wished me to be present also.

'In his car as we went to see Lord Loch, Lord Hurst told me that we were going to lunch at the Savoy Hotel in the restaurant at Table 3 at 1.15. We then went to see Lord Loch and Lord Hurst said: "When I first came to this country as a poor German boy my one ambition was to become a British citizen. It was beyond my imagination that I should ever become a Peer of the Realm and, in fact, that I would not be without the many friends of my company, of which you are one. I therefore came to thank you for this friendship and I wish you to know that there is nothing that I can do that Geffers cannot do. He is our ambassador in whom we have complete confidence and we hope you will too. He is the General Electric Company. I am here only to say thank you. He is in the best position to advise you." And having said this, he then turned to me saying: "And now Geffers, where do you take us for lunch?" I was able to follow my earlier instructions to the letter.

'In this way, my relationship with the Greyhound Racing Association, one of our largest customers, was completely assured and I was even more assiduous in my duties.'

11 Customer Service

Customer service is the last great frontier of marketing management. It has been the least glamorous area because it is not involved directly, or so it is thought, with the customer. So almost by definition it has escaped the attention of the marketing pundits. Yet customer service has probably produced, as a department, more members of top management than any other department. The 'office', as it has long been called, is the nerve centre of a business and, because of the range of services provided, enables anyone with the appropriate ambition to learn, with panoramic vision, the intricacies involved in all operational departments and, more importantly, how they interact with each other.

Although other activities of marketing still show signs of a rapid move towards improvements in productivity, little is heard of how customer service may be improved. Yet the customer service department is an essential aid to those other elements. Really significant improvements in total cannot be achieved without a commensurate reformation in the interacting function. Salesmen cannot develop their selling activities without the office absorbing routine tasks. Distribution cannot be improved without more effective stock control. Advertising will not bring real rewards unless enquiry handling is sharpened. Nor will growth be achieved without adequate attention being given to the major areas of customer service. It is giving attention to all these areas that results in the 'Total Marketing Concept'. Areas of customer service are:

1   Company service strategy
2   Credit control, allowances, returns, discounts, cancellations
3   Hire purchase, credit sales, leasing, factoring, franchising
4   After-sales service; installation, maintenance service, spare parts
5   Guarantees and warranties
6   Stock control
7   Telephone selling
8   Premiums, joint ventures
9   The sales office organisation
10   Enquiry handling
11   The sales supporting service
12   Management information, accounting, computers, operational research

All these elements are designed to be customer-orientated, although they could easily be mistaken for defensive or counter-offensive operational ploys. A few companies have shown how management can use these activities as positive aids to growth. They are worth considering in some detail.

1   Company service strategy

Too often companies dissipate their effort by trying to do too much and are therefore unable to do anything well. The truly efficient companies avoid the temptation to seize every little work opportunity that comes their way. They concentrate on doing what they do well and work hard at it. But what companies can do well is subject to considerable variety. However, the range can be grouped into six categories:

(a)   Full customer service
Here the company tries to cater for a group of customers' every needs. The nearest one can get to this ideal is the mail order

house that tries to offer a departmental store on display in every home.

(b) Limited product line specialist

This type of company produces basically one product and sells it primarily to one market. This is usually the function of the small firm, but it does happen in some big concerns such as breweries and aircraft manufacturers.

(c) Specific product specialist

In this example the company has one general-purpose product and markets it according to any preselected opportunity. Newspapers and magazines are good examples. Self-adhesive tape or lettering stencils are recent developments, while paper-makers are perhaps the best example.

(d) Market specialist

The company chooses a particular market and then tries to provide a comprehensive service. Burmah Oil may be quoted as an example since its acquisition of Halfords, Castrol and Quinton Hazell in order to provide a full service to the motorist.

(e) 'Specials' producers

Usually this company has some general-purpose machine that is capable of producing custom-specified goods. This is the province of the general engineering company, the jobbing printer or the plastics moulder.

(f) Product line specialist

Often these companies are suppliers of essential services, and in the UK they have mostly been nationalised. They include coal, gas, electricity, railways, postal and telephone services. If not wholly nationalised, they are usually involved in government-supported industries, such as oceanography or rocketry.

These are all strategic in nature but are in essence the first effort at marketing orientation. By implication they each dominate customer service—they are, in fact, customer-orientated, although the product dominates the strategy in more than one example. Yet even where the product must dominate the company, it is clear that customers are identified, clear benefits to them established and the product sold accordingly. In each case the supplier has aided its customers in the development of their markets.

2 Credit control, allowances, returns, discounts, cancellations

This is an area that more often than not is the centre of disruption between a company and its supplier. Clearly this must be avoided. But more than that it is a source of promotion. Each of the activities listed involves a contact, and with that contact an exchange of documents or correspondence. Moreover, each of these contacts means the transfer of money or credit. Whichever way the money moves there is scope for building goodwill. Clerks trained in customer service see each of these transactions as an opportunity to show courtesy, interest, consideration and efficiency. They are taught to write letters bursting with goodwill and co-operation, and they learn telephone techniques that reflect the image of a well-run personalised company.

This practice is adopted because it is good for the firm both internally and externally. It is good for the firm internally because it breeds morale and good externally because the executives who handle money matters are often the customer's senior management. But even these virtues will be of little avail if the company policy on these executives is too restrictive or, as frequently happens, is so indeterminate that a conscientious but unknowing middle manager implements traditional rulings that bear little relationship to today's needs. For example, one company in Scotland stopped buying from one source because the supplier would not accept the return on its own van of charged packages. The ruling had been made when crates were not charged and were delivered by rail. A valuable relationship was lost because no one thought of customer service whenever circumstances changed.

Suppliers will always receive complaints. If a company finds that it is satisfying everyone all the time, then the chances are that it is cheating itself in some way. It is probably giving too much away. As firms find that another concern is always capable of meeting their demands, then they tend to allow these demands to grow—not necessarily intentionally. It happens because pressures from all round force them to exploit the willing. When they are suddenly let down they blame the other party, not themselves. They make a complaint. It is at this moment that the opportunist supplier acts. He uses the handling of the complaint as a means to build goodwill. Normally the irate customer is well aware that he is being unreasonable, particularly if he has been allowed to let off steam. Properly handled, the complaint can be a major business builder. Some years ago in the essential oil business a buyer was always too busy to see a supplier's salesman. Purchases were small but steady. The salesman had a new line which he was confident the customer would buy in some volume—if only he could get in to see him. On receipt of a small order for an essence, the salesman collected the goods and carried them about in his car until the customer complained. Within three hours of the complaint—the timing was predictable because deliveries were made every fourteen days —the salesman was in the office of the buyer delivering the goods personally and collecting the planned order on the way out. The buyer did not ask why the goods had not been delivered as usual, he was too delighted at having his problem solved by this 'service-orientated' supplier.

3   Hire purchase, credit sales, leasing, factoring, franchising

As before, this aspect of customer service is involved with the movement of money, so all the remarks made earlier apply.

The impact that hire-purchase and credit-sale agreements have had on business is well documented. Frequently suppliers discover that by allowing terms they become part of the banking business. This has allowed them to increase their profit returns quite substantially—not because of exploitation but because it has enabled more people to buy; and it has also meant higher productivity of resources both because of the increase in volume and through earning a profit as a manufacturer and as a banker from the same transaction. Credit cards, cheque cards and money shops and their growing acceptance indicate an increasing move away from cash transactions. Firms are preparing for the day when all business is transacted on credit. Having the immediate use of a purchase negates the cost of the credit, particularly in days of continuing inflation.

Capital equipment firms have already marketed the advantages of leasing equipment. In effect the customers are sharing the costs of expertise involved in the running of the service. Whether it be a computer in industry or a television set in the home, the costs incurred are known and therefore predictable in the future. It is a form of insurance whereby the customer indemnifies himself against unusual occurrences. He buys a trouble-free service.

It has been estimated that 10% of the world's trade is now factored. The system may seem reminiscent of feudalism and of bartering on a huge scale, but it has won acceptance and is growing. Furthermore, it shows every sign of expansion as the world currency crisis develops. Firms anxious to grow in international markets are beginning to obtain comprehensive information sources on international trade to support their own selling efforts.

Franchising is rightly regarded as a channel of distribution. It is also a financial arrangement for the granting of a commercial privilege. It is not new—kings and rulers have granted franchises for centuries, and a 'by appointment' is a franchise to the depicted monarch.

Petrol stations and the British public house operate on a franchise provided by their suppliers. Perhaps the most notable franchise company of all is Coca-Cola, with business widely established throughout the world.

The major argument in favour of the franchise movement is the opportunity it creates for anyone to become his own boss. It is often cited as the new era of entrepreneurial activity. Quite clearly the system does allow a person to run his own business, at the same time enabling him to enjoy the advantages of belonging to a large corporation. For example, there are cafes and restaurants in most towns, but their quality of service and their prices cover a wide range. A Wimpy Bar, despite being privately owned, has a consistency of facilities, menu, quality and prices. Few people today need to study the menu outside before venturing in; they know the level for which the outlet provides.

Franchising has earned a bad reputation because some franchisers dished out franchises indiscriminately, taking the franchisee's investment and then allowing him to sink without help. Meanwhile, other franchisers, using pyramid selling, built up big distributive organisations through recruitment incentives which made it unnecessary to carry out the distribution of goods except by selling them as stock-in-trade to the franchisees. But in any new business development there will always be people looking for easy money and who may finish up being duped. Notwithstanding such human frailities, the system has many advantages to offer, both to the franchisee and to society and the economy as a whole. These are:

The franchisee   (*a*)   Has the vested interest of the entrepreneur.

(*b*)   Enjoys the benefits of full association with large operation.

(*c*)   Can obtain managerial advice and guidance.

(*d*)   Enjoys joint promotion and reputation.

(*e*)   Has a tried and proved system of operation.

The franchiser   (*a*)   Enjoys the self-motivation of the franchisee.

(*b*)   Expands his total distribution.

(*c*)   Limits his capital involvement.

(*d*)   Limits administrative problems involved.

Because both parties join their businesses together, the mutal benefits improve both firms' chances of success, with lowered investment risks, sounder decision-making and better use of joint resources. Perhaps the only real disadvantage of the system is that it may sometimes involve decisions made by the franchiser in the interests of the majority but which may be injurious to a few. All franchisees must ensure that they do not sign away real control of their business. For those individuals or organisations considering a franchise operation, the Institute of Marketing at Moor Hall publishes a check list available free.

4   After sales service; installation, maintenance, service, spare parts

Few companies have realised the growth potential that exists through the development of a first-class after-sales service promoted as a pre-sale incentive. Volkswagen grew in America because of the company's insistence on minimum standards of operation among its distributors. The conditions were so stringent that they amounted to a legal franchise of the sort described earlier. Despite the renowned success of the operation, few companies have adopted a similar approach. Building foundations for tomorrow do not seem to appear high on the list of company priorities, hence the dearth of planning systems and the reluctance to develop customer service.

Even so, there is no reason why the company's own service staff should not receive promotional training. Like the salesman, the service engineer is in frequent contact with the customer. Unlike the salesman, however, he has to deal with the people responsible for running the machine *who will not have been sold on the machine's potential, its benefits and the reasons for its original choice*. It may have caused redundancies, loss of earnings, demotion. In resentment the machine's operation could be 'spiked' (concealed sabotage). The new owners will blame the suppliers. Even if they don't, goodwill may be harmed. A good engineer trained to understand machine/people problems will attempt to sell the merits of the machine and take pride in showing his counterpart how to get the maximum benefit. Because he is an engineer he will tend to feel somewhat shamefaced about a second-hand or an inexpensive model. In an efficient company he is taught that customers know best and buy what suits them. He is shown that with a cheaper machine customers can make profits, while with a bigger, more sophisticated piece of equipment—perhaps his own pride and joy—they may make thumping great losses if it has more capacity than can be economically used.

In making a capital investment a company rates 'trouble-free' operation as highly as the average motorist, not just because servicing is expensive but because stopped machines make men idle, lower production, allow perishable raw materials to spoil and keep customers waiting. The resultant cost may be very high indeed. Building a reputation for 'trouble-free running' adds a premium value to the machine. Even if management does not acknowledge this real truth it is clear the trade unions have. They know the best time and place to strike.

In the motor car industry the manufacturers have jeopardised a substantial portion of their sales revenue by carrying limited stocks of spare parts—avoiding interchangeable parts is partly responsible for stock problems—and so allowing firms such as Quinton Hazell to sweep the cream off the market.

The rules adopted by service-orientated companies are:

(a) After-sales service is a sales *promotional* function.
(b) Installation is supplied in the price and expected to be fully and satisfactorily operational when the product is sold.
(c) Maintenance is the means of safeguarding the company's reputation.
(d) Service is the means of making a customer's investment pay.
(e) Spare parts are an integral part of a piece of equipment and extras will be supplied automatically prior to MTBF (Mean Time Before Failure).

Clearly there is scope for improvement in most companies. The need is so apparent that some companies are making a successful business out of safeguarding customers' needs by renting, or leasing, goods such as television sets, cars, etc. and are therefore providing a full free and efficient service.

4 Guarantees and warranties

All marketing transactions are subject to the Sale of Goods Act 1893, the Trade Descriptions Act 1965 and the Supply of Goods (Implied Terms) Act 1973 (see Chapter 5 on publicity).

In essence, these acts make all warranties worthless and unnecessary, except where the manufacturer wishes to make his guarantee better than the minimum requirements laid down by statute. This is so rare that, for most purposes, the consumer or user can safely ignore any implied advantage contained within an offer of a guarantee. However, it can be said that registering a purchase with a manufacturer, which is all that it amounts to, does help to ensure that the manufacturer will accept his responsibilities, almost without question, rather than insist on the purchaser making a proper claim and incurring the effort and expense involved.

Those manufacturers wishing to promote the reliability or trouble-free running of their goods or applicances could offer to prospects all the benefits under the relevant Acts and then identify and state specifically the additional facilities provided. All benefits should be stated categorically in terms relevant, as well as appealing, to the purchaser.

The new Supply of Goods (Implied Terms) Act May 1973 is a tightened up version of the earlier 1893 Act. In consequence, retailers will find it difficult to avoid their legal responsibility for the quality of things they sell and hence it could lead to the settlement of claims without litigation.

The practice of getting customers to sign away their rights under the old Act by the substitution of the manufacturer's own warranty is now largely ineffective. The new Act does not forbid exclusion clauses, but it does ensure that substituted conditions must be better than those provided for legally. There is, however, one loophole. If defects are brought to the buyer's attention before sale, the seller is protected. Furthermore, if any defects ought to have been revealed by examination, then the seller will have a good defence. Buyers are advised to use an independent witness willing to testify as to the extent or the thoroughness of any examination. For the customer-orientated company, it is wise to bring all defects or limitations to the prospects' attention so that he may judge for himself; presumably the item will have been priced for sale with all factors accounted for and thus a realistic price will have been established. Any such warning should always be confirmed in writing—and clearly so that the customer cannot claim to have been misled. A much better arrangement is for the seller to promote 'money back' guarantees.

5 Stock control

In studying the annual accounts of numerous firms it seems that many of them are carrying excessive stocks. Dividing the stock-held value into the sales revenue for two or more successive years shows average stocks valued at many months of sales. This is true of companies with delivery lead times of weeks rather than months. Yet no doubt these companies are confronted with constant stock-out problems. They all seem to face a conflict involving the desirable mix of stock items. The conflict is between the need to satisfy customers' demands and the necessity to produce in economic batch quantities. So the supplier faces a double problem: when to produce, and how much to produce? These conflicting interests need to be considered in more detail. The benefits of holding stock are:

- (*a*) Lower average unit costs of production
- (*b*) More efficient production programming
- (*c*) Better delivery timing
- (*d*) Avoidance of excess scrap

Clearly stock-holding provides a cushion for both the manufacturer and his customer. The limiting of risk that this entails is, moreover, additional to the higher productivity achievable from the system. The evaluation of each kind of benefit is made easier by further consideration.

(*a*) *Lower average unit costs of production*
By deciding economic batch quantities a company makes savings on each quantity made. The principle is similar to that applying to the theory of economies of scale. Machine set-up time is minimised, purchase order levels are realistic and timed, and, of course, the limiting factor of time is used to economic advantage.

(*b*) *More efficient production programming*
If goods are made to order, then not only will more general-

purpose machinery be required but also machines will be only partly used for production. More efficient production is achieved by running purpose-built machines at maximum capacity for long periods. By planning ahead the production manager is able to utilise the machines in this way by making for stock rather than dealing with each order as it arrives and deploying machines accordingly. This approach is particularly beneficial when goods have a seasonal demand. It is realised by the more progressive companies that limited output from machines must carry a higher rate of overhead per unit than units of mass production or economic production.

(c) Better delivery timing

Delivery is an inherent feature of a purchase just as much as price or product specification. Extended delivery may force a customer to seek compensation for remaining loyal. Clearly 'ex-stock' is a desirable benefit to offer prospects, particularly if delivery can be made almost instantly. There is little point in building up large stocks if the delivery service is poor. Customers judge by actual delivery, not by the ex-works state. In fact, there is nothing more infuriating to a customer than to know that his urgent needs are available at the factory but that the delivery van is not due for two weeks.

(d) Avoidance of excess scrap

Most products have a minimum output level. For example, a printer may offer to supply 100 printed leaflets, but his price will allow for the 400 that may be wasted. Not all firms are able to charge the realistic rate for small orders because they have no sensible means of knowing just what that rate is.

The disadvantages of holding stock are:

(a) The actual costs involved
(b) Limitation on providing flexibility

(a) The actual costs involved

These costs may be quite considerable. Moreover, there are numerous ways in which they are incurred:

    (i)   Cost of interest on capital tied-up
    (ii) Cost of the space
   (iii) Cost of shelving or special packaging
   (iv) Costs of damage or deterioration
    (v) Costs of pilferage
   (vi) Costs of insurance
  (vii) Costs of administration
 (viii) Costs of handling and labour
   (ix) Costs of obsolescence
    (x) Costs of lost opportunity

Although these are real costs, they apply equally at each stage in the channel of distribution, so for society as a whole the practice of keeping buffer stocks all the way down the line has a multiplier effect.

(b) Limitations on providing flexibility

Carrying stocks made in economic quantities forestalls the possibility of a company meeting individual customer requirements, since the cost of ad hoc orders becomes prohibitive. This means that the supplier is less likely to be attuned to changes in the market place.

Stock-holding is an area where nominal adherence to marketing principles is revealed. The marketing plan may specify concentration of effort on a growth sector of the market, offering products with growth potential to companies of a size capable of meeting the minimum order requirements. In practice the weaker company meets the requirements of everyone that sends in an order, fills unused capacity with whatever happens to turn up in the post and carries stock for the major accounts who 'would go elsewhere for their computers if they did not supply their pencils'. Under such action it is small wonder that 'marketing' opportunities are missed and marketing management considered unsuccessful.

7 Telephone selling

As we have seen earlier, personal calls by the salesman are expensive in both selling and non-selling time, besides which the limited time available to salesmen is best spent with customers who are substantial prospects and in the way that is most effective—personal contact. In a well-chosen territory with 100 prospects offering real potential, the salesman is fully occupied.

But there is much business available that does not justify the personal attention of the salesmen—after all, the mail order business thrives on a selling job carried out through the mail—and these prospects have to be cultivated. Some may be happy to send orders through the post, and for the very small account this is the ideal way of handling the business. On the other hand, some businesses require a more active approach, particularly if their trade is thriving. The sales effort in this case is often left to an inside salesman trained to use the telephone to its best advantage. The telephone has flexibility and a time-saving factor not realisable in either personal calls or postal communications.

Although the telephone is often used as a supplement to the salesman, it is sometimes used to complement his efforts. The inside salesman uses the phone to supplement his selling activity on low-priority calls and to complement his selling effort at desirable calls where the salesman may not be able to visit as often as he should. The system has become so sophisticated in some fields that a number of companies have achieved prominent market growth attributable to their use of telephone selling techniques. Examples are Golden Wonder, Birds Eye and Thompson Yellow Pages. The specific benefits attributable to the telephone are:

(a) Low cost of frequent contact.
(b) Is a time-saving factor for both parties.
(c) Provides a filter on potential of prospects.
(d) Can be used for promotions as well as order-sending.
(e) Enables the sales person to meet objections.
(f) Calls can be timed to meet customer needs.
(g) Helps to improve market coverage.
(h) Enables changes in price etc. to be conveyed immediately.
(i) Is a check on the salesman's performance.
(j) Enables high-calibre married women to be used more readily.
(k) Solicits real leads for salesmen.
(l) Allows re-call during times of pressure.
(m) Makes use of standardised sales presentation possible.

These points make the use of the telephone a formidable promotional weapon and one that has considerable potential for all companies. Its blessing is that it is entirely modular and so allows big things to develop from small beginnings.

8 Premiums and joint ventures

The premiums promotions business has yet to get over its 'daffodil'. The scope for the promotional method is high. Many items if manufactured in bulk, perhaps in a once-off order, can be produced at a price significantly cheaper than if produced and marketed in a slow-moving market. Often the significant costs may be in distribution, and where 'carried' by some other item the additional costs may be minimal. In this way a manufacturer is often able to make premium offers for goods valued at £1 for, perhaps, 25 pence. Special offers of this sort enable firms to provide excellent value for money to the consumer. And no one loses anything because an unexploited market has been tapped. As a promotional technique the premium promotion is particularly useful for:

(*a*) Introducing a new product.

(*b*) Extending an existing market.

(*c*) Increasing usage.

(*d*) Building 'trade' goodwill.

(*e*) Special sales campaigns.

(*f*) Increasing order value.

(*g*) Weakening competitive activity.

(*h*) Monitoring publicity campaigns.

One of the hidden benefits of running a premium promotion is the direct contact this introduces to the manufacturer. Apart from anything else it provides the concern with a mailing list, with which future promotion activity may be undertaken and used as a control document. But premium promotions are joint ventures. Joint ventures provide another useful channel of distribution, but equally they provide a means by which a company may extend the area of its service so prohibiting the growth of competitors.

9 The sales office organisation

Although the services provided by most offices tend to be similar, they are often organised in different ways:

(*a*) Functional organisation

(*b*) Product-based organisation

(*c*) Market-based organisation

(*d*) Area-based organisation

(*e*) Integrated office organisation.

The organisation adopted by the firm is usually dependent on its corporate strategy—the means by which its marketing operation is implemented. As the office is usually the nerve centre of the business, further consideration of the different organisations is necessary.

(*a*) *Functional organisation*

In this category an employee or group of employees performs

the same function for all company products or sales. These functions will include handling inquiries, pricing, sampling, stock records, estimating, credit control, tendering, progress chasing and costing. Each employee must be sufficiently versatile to handle the range of tasks for which he or she is responsible.

(b) Product-based organisation

In this type of organisation staff are recruited with 'product' knowledge, with each section largely self-sufficient and responsible for a particular product or group of products.

(c) Market-based organisation

The staff in this organisation are divided up into sections, with each section responsible for a specific market, usually distinguished by a particular class of outlet. In this type of organisation the staff will be expected to have sound knowledge of the operational structure and procedures for the class of outlet for which they are responsible.

(d) Area-based organisation

This type of organisation may be any permutation of the above, but with its geographical areas divided into territories capable of easy handling by office staff.

(e) Integrated office services

The acceptance of computers and data processing has tended to break down departmental walls and so it is no longer necessary for the sales office to be separated from accounts or purchasing. In this organisation the office is fully integrated, with an office manager providing expertise in record-keeping, transcription and management information systems.

10 Enquiry handling

Every customer first became a customer as a result of an enquiry. Every customer wanting additional goods or services makes an enquiry. Every enquiry is a business opportunity. It is an organisation looking for supplies and prepared to pay for them. If business does not result from an enquiry, it must be because the supplier did not want the business. It should not, as so often happens, be by default. Many firms lose business because they do not respond adequately to the invitation. Either they delay replying or they do not trouble to establish the enquirers real needs. While it is true that some firms will send out circular letters in the search for suppliers (indicating that something is wrong with the supplier's promotional efforts), it is more usual for a prospect to make contact with one of his established suppliers, possibly the salesman, and ask whether they know of a source. Because his reputation is at stake the supplier will recommend a firm known to him as reliable and efficient. Judgment will be based on what other customers have reported.

The only golden rules for enquiry handling are: use a system and make one person responsible, and issue a definite policy and procedure with monitoring of progress and results. And remember that many enquiries start with the telephone operator.

11 The sales supporting service

In the chapters covering the salesman and sales management it was emphasised that, because of the real cost of face-to-face selling time, considerable improvements in productivity may be achieved if the salesman is helped in the performance of his more routine functions. So apart from the sales office carrying out many routine calls by telephone, the clerical staff can be helpful in obtaining and supplying useful information to the salesman and his customers.

12 Management information, accounting, computers, operational research

While modern management techniques have been widely documented as aids to cost effectiveness, it is often forgotten that improvements in operating efficiency also benefit the customer.

Sales analysis may well indicate trends in market movements. Such information could be vital to a customer struggling to decide where to invest his capital for growth. Similarly, accounting information such as return on capital employed or return on sales could suggest more profitable opportunities, yet unknown to customers. This could be particularly true if it is discovered that customers are losing money because they are aiming for a high margin, so prohibiting growth. Co-operating with customers and supplying them 'below cost' until economies of scale are achieved could prove a wise investment compared with a heavy marketing campaign. Furthermore, computerisation, mathematical models and/or operational research techniques can be, and are sometimes, used to bring benefits to customers. Improving delivery schedules may often bring more rewards than reducing the operating costs of deliveries. This is true market- or customer-orientation. Using quantitative techniques often results in better decision-making data; they will be as vital to the future of marketing as qualitative techniques have been in the past.

12 Marketing as a Career

Marketing practice provides opportunities for all interested members of society, whether male or female, skilled or unskilled, educated or not so well educated. Once started in marketing, progress is more dependent on ability at the job than may be true of other functions. Certainly marketing practitioners choose their own level, whether consciously or subconsciously. One of the deciding factors, of course, is the level of education reached either by graduation, post-graduation or post-experience. While education is not an essential factor, even today, nevertheless for the majority it is as good as essential.

There are a number of learned bodies that provide the means by which students acquire the necessary level of knowledge and skills. One is the Institute of Marketing, Moor Hall, Cookham, Berkshire. Over the past fifteen years the Institute has clearly established a lead in the UK in its education and training policies by minimising the operation of 'flair' in management ability. It has developed its own courses in the belief that business problems arise as a result of specific applied techniques, together with the application of systematic method developed through application and practice. It does not pretend that its courses can produce good managers, but it does believe that good managers become better managers as a result of the technique taught being put into practice.

The Diploma in Marketing

The Diploma examination is a prime example. Graduates are not simply made familiar with a loose string of separate management disciplines, they are trained to do a job of work and to use the education they have acquired in dealing with practical situations. The Marketing III case-study examination fully expresses this technique and is unique in its form and application. The revised examination syllabus now being introduced goes even further. It provides students with a fairly rigourous course of study, and examines them finally by application. Moreover, it gives them a thorough grasp of the principles of quantitative measurement, on the one hand, and an appreciation of social psychology, on the other. They will thus be equipped with the most significant tools of practising managers, together with the means to apply them, and new techniques where older methods have proved inadequate.

One of the continuing problems facing the Institute in its marketing education programme is the numerous definitions of the term 'marketing'. While IM has its own official definition, it recognises the inadequacy of any single version. Each tends to be too vague to give any real insight into methodology and yet encompass all that its practitioners accomplish. However, IM holds the belief that marketing is *the* dynamic element in management, and by its creative effect compels increasing attempts at improvements in management philosophy and in the co-ordination of established practices of an inter-functional kind. So marketing has become the discipline for top management, particularly in the area of business strategy.

So marketing education in the UK, under the auspices of the Institute of Marketing, has been founded on the assembly of a body of knowledge developed from rational first principles related to the practices of leading companies throughout the world, prepared in a form suitable for teaching and which, when applied correctly, will help to improve the operating efficiency of a trading organisation.

The essence of marketing is in the gathering together of relevant information, the development of a model capable of generating forecasts and predictions, and the co-ordination of resultant product plans and communication policies which, suitably managed, form the basis for changing consumer behaviour patterns in pursuit of predetermined objectives.

The coverage essential to satisfy essential minimum standards of knowledge and skill acquisition required by the Institute of Marketing is quite specific.

Aims of the Diploma course

1 To enable the student to reach a level of knowledge adequate for a decision on the employment or otherwise of a marketing specialist.

2 To give the graduate an overall view of the marketing function sufficient to enable him to brief and to monitor professional services whenever required.

3 To provide the student with a full appreciation of the factors which, gathered together, form the basis of 'services' to customers and so provide the means by which product policies are developed.

4 To establish in the student an instinctive orientation towards customer satisfaction within the bounds of a fully economic operation.

5 To encourage the graduate to think in marketing terms when considering any business decision and particularly when approaching financial problems—specifically in the areas of investment and operation.

6 To form the basis for subsequent study of marketing methods and management in chosen industries or other national environments.

7 To prepare the student for a successful and rewarding career in any of the marketing functions leading to a

marketing management position, and for subsequent promotion into general management.

Over 100 colleges and polytechnics provide courses which lead to the examinations for the Diploma. Apart from the usual three-year course, it is possible first to obtain an HNC or an HND in Business Studies and then to take the final year examinations for the Institute's diploma. As well as normal evening class study, day facilities at the time of writing are available at establishments in Bristol, Dublin, Liverpool, London, Luton, Middlesborough, Sheffield and Slough.

Correspondence courses are provided by the Rapid Results College, the Metropolitan College and International Correspondence Schools. These courses are well designed and constructed, and are particularly useful to those students unable to attend a college due to travelling problems or because their occupation does not allow them the freedom to attend a regular fixed-time course. All these correspondence courses are approved by the Institute of Marketing.

The educational facilities provided by the Institute are the envy of many other other professional associations. The Marketing 111 paper, which is problem-orientated, is a typical example. It consists of a paper in which a candidate is expected to apply his knowledge and understanding of technique to the appraisal of business situations. The paper offers a single case-study. The examinee is required to examine the facts and to apply his theoretical knowledge, as well as his experience in offering reasoned solutions to the problems set. All candidates receive a copy of the case-study, upon which the examination is based, at least one month before the date of the examination. They are then expected to analyse and interpret the information in preparation for the examination, which normally consists of one question relevant to the case-study.

The standard expected of students is of degree level and, in fact, the Institute expects entrants to have achieved an academic level consistent with university entry prior to registration. It does, however, allow the older student, over twenty-five years of age, to register provided that he or she is suitably employed in a marketing position and has the full support of an employer. The Diploma in Marketing is recognised by the Department of Education and Science as of pass degree standard.

Many graduates sit the Diploma examinations as a post-graduate qualification. Although it is accepted by the Institute that the award of the Diploma could never signify management competence, since the complete measurement of executive performance is beyond the scope of a formal examination, it does provide evidence that the holder has persuaded the examiners that he or she has acquired a broad and liberal education in marketing.

As the Council of the Institute plans to make graduation the normal means of entry to full membership, and the student registrations are close to those of the mature entrant, the future of the body seems assured and augurs well for British industry, which has not yet shown itself to be truly marketing-orientated.

The Institute sponsored the first Chair in Marketing at Lancaster University, providing an MA in Marketing as a one-year, post-experience or post-graduate award.

Other universities and colleges of technology offer courses with an emphasis on marketing, ranging from a nine-month MSc. course at Strathclyde to a three-year course leading to a BA Textile Marketing at Huddersfield. There are four-year courses (CNAA) for a BA Business Studies, with marketing as an option.

Perhaps one of the best-known colleges providing courses in marketing is the College for the Distributive Trades, Leicester Square, London. CDT is unique in having the only department in any educational establishment in the UK devoted entirely to marketing and advertising education. Details of the main courses in marketing subjects offered by CDT are given here.

Courses offered by the Department of Marketing and Advertising
Studies at the College for Distributive Trades

Guide to courses, entry requirements and qualifications gained

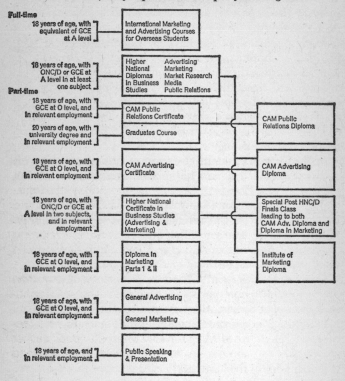

Full-time

18 years of age, with equivalent of GCE at A level — International Marketing and Advertising Courses for Overseas Students

18 years of age, with ONC/D or GCE at A level in at least one subject — Higher National Diplomas in Business Studies / Advertising, Marketing, Market Research, Media, Public Relations

Part-time

18 years of age, with GCE at O level, and in relevant employment — CAM Public Relations Certificate

20 years of age, with university degree and in relevant employment — Graduates Course

→ CAM Public Relations Diploma

18 years of age, with GCE at O level, and in relevant employment — CAM Advertising Certificate → CAM Advertising Diploma

18 years of age, with ONC/D or GCE at A level in two subjects, and in relevant employment — Higher National Certificate in Business Studies (Advertising & Marketing) → Special Post HNC/D Finals Class leading to both CAM Adv. Diploma and Diploma in Marketing

18 years of age, with GCE at O level, and in relevant employment — Diploma in Marketing Parts 1 & II → Institute of Marketing Diploma

18 years of age, with GCE at O level, and in relevant employment — General Advertising / General Marketing

18 years of age, and in relevant employment — Public Speaking & Presentation

Note: All classes start in September, other than the Higher National Certificate course, which has a second intake in January.

Details of some of these courses are given below. Students are advised to study these carefully to select the course best suited to their qualifications and career intentions. The College will be pleased to advise students in this respect.

FULL-TIME COURSES

Title of Course **Higher National Diplomas in Business Studies**

Duration 2 years

Objective These two-year full-time courses prepare students broadly for the fields of advertising, marketing and public relations, and also provide opportunity for students to have some degree of specialisation according to their specific career intentions.

Subjects studied There is a common first year in which the subjects are Economics, Media, Advertising Administration, Advertisement Design, Copywriting, and Print and Production. During the first year students also pursue general studies, including Statistics, Law, Sociology and Public Speaking.

In the second year there is a common core of three subjects: Applied Economics, Marketing and Market Research. Students select additional subjects, according to their interests and career intentions, to take one of the following five Options:

> Advertising Studies
> Marketing
> Market Research
> Media
> Public Relations

Additional subjects from which students

can select include Human Relations,
Statistics and Data Processing, Advanced Copywriting and Design,
Business Finance, Media Evaluation and
Planning, and Public Relations. Selection of subsidiary subjects, and thus
final vocational choice, is made only
after students have had the benefit of a
full year's study. During the second year,
students are placed with firms, according to their career intentions, to gain
working experience as part of their
course. There are minimum national
standards for the examinations, and for
attendance and written work throughout
the course. Before admission to the
examinations, students must have pur-
sued the prescribed course ot study to
the satisfaction of the College.

**Award at end
of courses**   The courses lead to the Higher National
Diploma in Business Studies, a qualification recognised by the Department of
Education and Science. They are also an
official route to the respective examinations of the Communication, Advertising
and Marketing Education Foundation,
the Institute of Marketing and the
Institute of Public Relations, and College
HND students can proceed direct to the
Final diplomas of these professional
bodies. The HND also admits students
to the Diploma in Management Studies.
Award of the Higher National Diploma is
made after students have gained at least
twelve months' business or administra-

tive experience after leaving the College.
Entry level Applicants must satisfy the Head of
Department that they are likely to benefit
from the courses. They must be 18 years
of age and hold the Ordinary National
Certificate or Diploma in Business
Studies, or have passed the General Certificate of Education (or some equivalent
examination) at Advanced level in at
least one suitable subject. In exceptional
cases, students over 21 who do not
possess these qualifications can be
admitted to the course if they can satisfy
the Head of Department of their ability
to profit from the course and complete it
satisfactorily.

PART-TIME COURSES

The Department offers a wide range of
part-time courses in the field of Advertising, Marketing and Public Relations.
These courses, listed below in approximate order from introductory to professional final level, are:

Diploma in Marketing
CAM Public Relations Certificate
CAM Advertising Certificate
HNC in Business Studies (Advertising
   and Marketing)
Graduates Course
CAM Advertising Diploma
Post HNC/D Finals

Title	**Diploma in Marketing**
Objective	To prepare students for the examinations of the Institute of Marketing .
Duration	3 years.
Entry level	Students must have passed General Certificate of Education at Ordinary level (or some equivalent examination) in at least four subjects, one of which must be English Language, and must be engaged in some form of marketing activity.
Minimum age	18
Subjects	Part 1: Marketing, Business Organisation, Economics, Statistics.
Awards	Diploma of the Institute of Marketing.
Registration	Prospective students are advised to write to the College before the official enrolment date for application form.
Cost	£6 (day) or £3 (half-day and evening) a year.
Special notes	(1) Students are required to enrol for all subjects in each Part and to pass the examinations in these subjects before proceeding to the next part. Evidence of passing must be produced when attending for enrolment. Any special case will be considered individually by the Head of Department.
	(2) There are minimum standards for attendance and written work throughout the course for students who wish to sit with the College as their Examination

Centre. Students who fail in these respects may be required to withdraw from the course.

(3) All students should, before enrolment, be registered with the Institute of Marketing.

(4) College HNC/D students taking Part III should enrol in the special post-HNC/D class below.

Title **CAM Public Relations Certificate**

Objective To prepare students for the Public Relations Certificate examinations of the Communication, Advertising and Marketing Education Foundation.

Duration 2 or 3 years.

Entry level Students must on entry be employed full-time in Public Relations and hold one of the following educational qualifications:

(a) General Certificate of Education at Advanced level in at least one approved subject.

(b) General Certificate of Education at Ordinary level in at least five subjects (including English).

Minimum age 18.

Subjects Business Organisation, Marketing, Public Relations, Media (PR Serviced and Directed), Human Relations, Production.

Class times **New students**
For new students, the College offers the CAM PR Certificate Course in two ways:

Half-day-with-evenings, over 2 years
The three subjects of Business Organisation, Marketing and Human Relations will be covered as follows:

Monday 1.30–5.30 and 6.15–8.15

Evenings-only, usually over 3 years
The PR Certificate Course comprises six subjects, and the College recommends that evenings-only students attempt two subjects per year. Any special cases will be considered individually by the Head of Department. First year subjects must include Business Organisation and Marketing which will be offered as follows:

Business Organisation	Monday	6.15–8.15
Marketing	Thursdays	6.15–8.15

Students are expected to attend on both evenings.

Continuing students
Continuing students wishing to take further subjects should have passed all previous subjects, and evidence of passing must be produced when attending for enrolment. Any special cases will be considered individually by the Head of Department.

Half-day-with-evenings

Production, Human Relations and Media (PR)	Monday	1.30–5.30 and 6.15–8.15

Evenings only
The College recommends that evenings-only students attempt two subjects per year. Any special cases will be considered individually by the Head of Department.

Marketing	Thursday	6.15–8.15
Human Relations	Monday	6.15–8.15
Production	Tuesday	6.15–8.15
or	Wednesday	6.15–8.15
Media (PR)	Thursday	6.15–8.15

Awards CAM Public Relations Cerificate

Registration Prospective students are advised to write to the college before the official enrolment date, for an application form.

Cost £3 (halfday–with evening) ⎱ each year
£2 (each evening) ⎰

Special notes (1) In *exceptional* cases only, students over 19 with at least three years relevant experience and others who can satisfy the College of their ability to profit by and complete the course satisfactorily, can be admitted at the discretion of the Head of Department.

(2) There are minimum standards for attendance and written work throughout the course for students who wish to sit with the College as their Examination Centre. Students who fail in these respects may be required to withdraw from the course.

(3) All students should before enrolment be registered with the Communication, Advertising and Marketing Education Foundation.

(4) All students should be in the appropriate grade of membership of the Institute of Public Relations before entering for the examinations, to ensure candidates accept the PR Code of Conduct.

Title   **CAM Advertising Certificate**

Objective   To prepare students for the Advertising Certificate Examination of the Communication, Advertising and Marketing Education Foundation.

Duration   2 or 3 years.

Entry level   Students must on entry be employed in the field of communication, advertising and marketing and hold one of the following educational qualifications:
(a) General Certificate of Education at Advanced level in at least one approved subject. See also Higher National Certificate entry below.
(b) General Certificate of Education at Ordinary level in at least five subjects, including English.

Minimum age   18.

Subjects   Business Organisation, Marketing, Advertising, Market Research, Media, Copywriting and Design, Production.

Class times   **New Students**
For new students, the College offers the CAM Advertising Certificate course in three ways:

Day-release, over 2 years

The three subjects of Advertising, Business Organisation and Marketing will be covered as follows:
    Friday   9.15–12.30 and 1.30–4.30

Half-day-with-evening, over 2 years
The three subjects of Advertising. Business Organisation and Marketing will be covered as follows:
    Monday   1.30–5.30 and 6.15–8.15
or Tuesday 1.30–5.30 and 6.15–8.15

Evenings-only, usually over 3 years
The Advertising Certificate Course comprises seven subjects and the College recommends evenings-only students not to attempt more than three subjects in any one year. The course thus involves two years in which two subjects are taken, and one in which three subjects are taken. The three-subject year can be the first, second or third year of study, as convenient for the student. First subjects must include Advertising and Business Organisation.

Continuing Students
Continuing students wishing to take further subjects should have passed all previous subjects and evidence of passing must be produced when attending for enrolment. Any special cases will be considered individually by the Head of Department. For continuing students, the College is offering the four subjects

of Production, Media, Market Research and Copy & Design.

Awards   CAM Advertising Certificate.

Registration   Prospective students are advised to write to the College before the official enrolment date for an application form.

Cost   £6 (full day)
£3 (half-day-with-evening) } each year.
£2 (each evening)

Special notes   (1) In *exceptional* cases only, students over 19 with at least three years relevant experience and others who can satisfy the College of their ability to profit by and complete the course satisfactorily can be admitted at the discretion of the Head of Department.

(2) There are minimum standards for attendance and written work throughout the course for students who wish to sit with the college as their Examination Centre. Students who fail in these respects may be required to withdraw from the course.

(3) All students should before enrolment be registered with the Communication, Advertising and Marketing Education Foundation.

(4) Students having General Certificate of Education at Advanced level in two subjects should consider the Higher National Certificate Course, below.

Title **CAM Public Relations Diploma**

Objective To prepare students for the Final Public Relations Diploma of the Communication, Advertising and Marketing Education Foundation, and Institute of Public Relations.

Duration 1 year.

Entry level Must be employed in Public Relations and have passed, or be otherwise exempt from, the CAM Public Relations Certificate.

Subjects Course content is still under consideration by CAM and the IPR.

Awards Public Relations Diploma of the Communication, Advertising and Marketing Education Foundation, and Institute of Public Relations.

Registration Prospective students are advised to write to the College before the official enrolment date for an application form.

Special notes (1) There are minimum standards for attendance and written work throughout the course for students who wish to sit with the College as their examination centre. Students who fail in these respects may be required to withdraw from the course.
(2) All students should, before enrolment, be registered with the CAM Education Foundation.
(3) All students should be in the appropriate grade of membership of the Institute of Public Relations before

entering for the examinations, to ensure candidates accept the IPR Code of Conduct.

Title   **CAM Advertising Diploma**

Objective   To prepare students for the Final Advertising Diploma examinations of the Communication, Advertising and Marketing Education Foundation (which have replaced the old Final examinations of the Advertising Association and the Institute of Practitioners in Advertising).

Duration   1 year.

Entry level   Must be employed in advertising and marketing and hold either:
(a) The CAM Advertising Certificate.
(b) Higher National Certificate or Diploma in Business Studies (Advertising and Marketing). College HNC/D students should enrol on the special post-HNC/D class below.

Subjects   General background of Advertising, Advertising and Marketing Abroad, and Advertising and Marketing problem analsis and Campaign planning.

Awards   Advertising Diploma of the Communication, Advertising and Marketing Education Foundation.

Registration   Prospective students are advised to write to the College before the official enrolment date for an application form.

Cost   £3 (day); £4 (2 evenings).

Special notes   (1) There are minimum standards for

attendance and written work throughout the course for those who wish to sit with the College as their examination centre. Students who fail in these respects may be required to withdraw from the course. (2) All students should, before enrolment, be registered with the CAM Education Foundation.

Title **Post-HNC/D Finals**

Objective To prepare suitably qualified students for both the CAM Advertising Diploma and Part III of the Diploma of the Institute of Marketing.

Duration 1 Year.

Entry level Enrolment on this course is retricted to those students who have previously gained their Higher National Certificate or Diploma (Advertising & Marketing) at the College.

Minimum age 20.

Subjects Marketing Case Studies, Industrial and Consumer Campaign Planning, International Advertising and Marketing.

Class times Thursday 1.30–5.30 and 6.15–8.15.

Awards Diploma of the Institute of Marketing, and Advertising Diploma of the CAM Education Foundation.

Registration Students are advised to write to the College before the official enrolment date for an application form.

Cost £3.

Special note   All students before enrolment should be registered with the Institute of Marketing and/or CAM Education Foundation.

Title   **Higher National Certificate in Business Studies (Advertising and Marketing)**

Objective   To prepare students for the Higher National Certificate examinations in Business Studies (Advertising and Marketing). See special note 1 below.

Duration   2 years. See special note 4 below.

Entry level   For acceptance on the course, students must hold one of the following educational qualifications:

(a) Ordinary National Certificate or Diploma in Business Studies.
(b) General Certificate of Education at Advanced level in two subjects directly related to business studies.
(c) Conversion Course. Students over 21 who have completed a suitable Conversion Course can be admitted to HNC.

Minimum age   18.

Subjects   Year 1: Applied Economics, Advertising I (Administration and Media), Advertising II (Design, Copywriting and Production).
Year II: Applied Economics, Marketing, Research.

Awards   Higher National Certificate in Business

Studies (Advertising and Marketing). Special note 1 below.

Registration Prospective students are advised to write to the College before the official enrolment date for an application form. See special note 4 below.

Cost Full day: £6
Half-day with evening £3 } each year.

Special notes (1) This two-year course is recognised as an official route to the Diploma of the Communication Advertising and Marketing Education Foundation and students can proceed direct to the CAM final examination. It also exempts from Part I and II of the examinations of the Institute of Marketing and HNC students can thus enter direct for Part III of the Diploma in Marketing. There is a special post-HNC/D class to prepare students for both these examinations. HNC also admits students to the Diploma in Management Studies.

(2) There are minimum national standards for the examinations, and for attendance and written work throughout the course.

(3) In exceptional cases only, students over 25 who do not possess the educational qualifications listed above can be admitted at the discretion of the Head of Department.

(4) The main course starts in September each year, but there is a second intake in January for those who are too late to join the September course.

13 A Case Study

In 1973 Ayala Designs Limited was awarded the Lord Mayor of London's Marketing Award. The winning submission, which was written by the author of this book, is reproduced here as a practical guide to marketing in action.

Ayala Designs Limited—Marketing in Belgium

Ayala Designs Limited was formed in 1966 to provide traditional English pubs for erection overseas. The founders had established that visitors from abroad invariably asked to be shown the old English pub rather than, say, the Old Vic or Covent Garden.

In developing its marketing plan for penetrating Europe, the company established a number of clear objectives, which included a forecast of anticipated sales volume, the share of the company manufacturing and design capacity to be devoted to each European country, and the growth targets which it could expect to achieve over a period of five years.

Formulating this data enabled the management to decide what action must be taken to establish its position in each area and to expand at the required rate, together with the resources required to develop its plans after initial entry.

Even at this early stage the company was working closely with a small reputable marketing consultancy. It was felt worthwhile to pay for outside help in order to obtain the benefits of time, contacts, organisation and expertise. Recognising many of the problems it would have to face, the company set out to establish itself in one prime market area, partly to resolve any resultant operational problems and partly owing to the influence of preliminary research findings, which indicated high potential in one country—Belgium. The management agreed that it would be better to enter one market where conditions were favourable, and to devote the firm's major marketing effort to that market. Other areas could then be developed as a result of established strength in a territory.

Information on the Belgian market was obtained from published sources such as the Readers' Digest *Products and People European Survey*, the then Westminster Bank *These Are Your Markets* series, the IPC Marketing Manual, and a number of published pieces provided by the Department of Trade and Industry (the BOT). In addition, the company used the files of its marketing consultant, together with an accumulation of information gleaned from various supporters in the hierarchy of a few British brewers.

Information sources revealed that the Belgians had a long-established taste for British-brewed beer. They had a growing preference for the top-fermented style rather than for the traditional continental lager. In addition, British brewers such as Watneys, Bass Charrington and Whitbread were clearly established in the country and some of their executives were looking at Belgium as a means of opening up the Common Market of which it was felt, even in 1967 and 1968, that the UK would inevitably become a member. Certainly these far-sighted managers welcomed the marketing stimulus that would clearly come from building old English-style pubs throughout Europe.

The Belgians are among the world's leading beer drinkers. Production figures in thousands of hectolitres have been (as prepared in 1967/68:

	Pop. (millions)	1953	1961	1962	1963	1964	1965	1966	1967 Est
Belgium	(10)	10 210	10 514	10 309	10 734	11 330	11 092	11 278	11 750
France	(50)	8 396	18 154	18 205	17 850	20 252	19 795	20 220	21 000
Germany	(60)	26 677	51 492	55 156	59 156	66 521	67 439	70 206	71 250
Italy	(54)	1 342	3 055	3 779	3 689	4 268	4 547	5 179	5 500
UK	(56)	40 888	45 333	45 660	46 315	48 442	49 442	49 424	50 000
Luxembourg	(·3)	366	446	448	471	519	512	542	550
Netherlands	(13)	1 832	3 802	3 965	4 408	4 965	5 402	5 695	6 000
Denmark	(5)	2 768	4 060	4 432	4 768	5 057	4 916	5 561	5 750
Ireland (Rep.)	(3)	3 036	3 622	3 461	3 396	3 463	3 466	3 478	3 500

So although imports/exports would alter these production figures in consumption terms (quite considerably in the case of Ireland where Guinness is made), there is a clear indication of the Belgian's cultivated taste for beer. Although the Germans' per capita consumption is higher, the market also is much greater and this could have meant a dissipation of the company's limited selling effort over a wider target area. It was also believed that Germans were unlikely to have quite the same nostalgia for British pubs and beer which the Belgians had already clearly indicated. It was estimated that approximately 10% of beer consumed was 'British-style', although some was home-produced, for Belgian imports in 1967/68 were thought to be less than 7% of total consumption.

The brewing industry in Belgium is highly fragmented. Many of the 40 000 sites identified as potential to Ayala are tied-houses, operating in a similar way to the British system. And as in the UK, it is distribution which is the key to the brewers' prosperity. Ayala's prestige outlets average £60 000, while the smaller grade B/C outlets average £20 000 per annum, estimated at 10% to 15% higher than traditional pubs. It was felt that this percentage would produce the bulk of profits for each outlet as well as for the supplying brewer; overheads and distribution costs figure so significantly in the operations of pub and brewer respectively that small increases in volume are likely to produce high profit ratios.

In choosing Belgium as its initial and prime target, Ayala accounted for its compactness and geographical area, and for the fact that approximately 25% of its population is concentrated in the four major cities of Brussels, Antwerp, Ghent and Liege.

This meant that every outlet would have a concentrated impact, that its appeal could spread over heavy population areas and that the company's early selling effort and expenditure could be devoted to best targets. Of some additional significance was the fact that more foreign countries have European headquarters in Belgium than anywhere else on the continent, with the exception of Switzerland. Belgium is easily the current favourite. And since Brussels houses the European Economic Community Commission (HQ of the Common Market) its significance as a central European city was clear. So the management held the view that success in Belgium would be more readily spread throughout Europe and the world as a result. The Belgians are classified as natively shrewd and, as a result, have developed a considerable national earning and purchasing power. Ayala management was aware that the country was considered an ideal test market and was frequently used by international companies for that purpose. Yet the country has limited home industries and it relies for much of its trade on overseas manufacturers. The Belgians are continually faced with a wide variety of products and they have become quite discriminating in their tastes. And legislation exists to prohibit restrictive practices 'against the public interest'.

Irrespective of whether exporting firms tend to provide a good service to their customers, ultimately purchasing decisions will often depend on what individual countries think is the service they will get. Therefore it was important for Ayala to establish in advance just what the Belgians were likely to believe and what preconceived ideas had to be overcome. Fortunately, there is a report which helps to clarify this problem. In 1963 the Reader's Digest undertook identical surveys of Common Market countries and Great Britain. As part of this survey, suitably updated in 1967, a cross-selection of adults were asked to express their opinions about the reputations of products from various countries. Extracted from table 46 of the report are the following rankings:

	Belgium	France	West Germany	Italy	Netherlands
High quality	4th	4th	2nd	4th	2nd
Reasonable price	8th	8th	8th	8th	8th
Modern design	7th	7th	7th	6th	7th
Well made, durable	2nd	2nd	1st	3rd	3rd

The extract is from a table showing how British products are rated in the Common Market as compared with those from France, West Germany, Italy, Sweden, Denmark, Belgium, the United States and Japan. It is significant that Great Britain was considered the least reasonably priced.

Other data considered were total population for each country, work force, wage and salary earners, unemployment, percentage of women as workers and a split of workers between industry, agriculture and services. In addition, figures showing relative income levels in terms of gross national product per head of population and average income per person. The major source of this information was ECSO.

Early in its deliberations the company had recognised the potential value to British brewers of its venture. So almost from the start the company's products became part of the Watneys major marketing operation in the country. In 1966 Watneys had become a local brewer by acquiring the 'top fermentation possibilities' of the Delbruyere Group near Charleroi. Watneys' estimates of Belgian demand for English-style beers may now be considered ahead of their time, but after it had acquired and merged the Vandenheuvel Group, Brussels, and the Maes concern in 1969 it had developed a better understanding of the then current market needs and the product mix necessary to satisfy those needs. Watneys now has an estimated 7% of the Belgian market. In the intervening years the company gave full support to Ayala in the establishment of new outlets and the refurbishing of old ones. Around 70% of new business for Ayala comes from these satisfied clients, and usually three out of five enquiries materialise into orders, indicating the success of the company's policy of prompt attention to enquiries. Currently the firm is erecting two outlets a month, each of which has an average value of £12 000.

Although the success of the operation has exceeded all expectations, the management is satisfied that it was correct in establishing a full marketing plan for the venture. Because much of the time still remains, only some outline details of the plan are publishable. First, the company documented clear objectives for the project. These objectives were expressed in monetary terms and included sales, volume and profit targets, together with operational budgets in detail. In developing the details of the plan the company produced figures for the number of enquiries to be sought, and from whom; the expected number and value of quotations which would be made against these enquiries; the anticipated number and value of resultant orders; and the sales that would be made. In setting these targets the management predicted conversion ratios for enquiries to quotations, quotations to orders, orders to sales and, critically, sales to profits. In retrospect, these conversion ratios all proved conservative, but they did, in fact, give the company clear yardsticks against which to work and by which actual results could be monitored. The management now believes that normal expectations were beaten because everyone worked to achieve the requirements of the plan and, because the factors all proved modest, pre-set goals were exceeded.

But the company did more than just establish targets. It also worked out strategies as to how each prediction could be achieved. In doing so it had to develop profiles of potential customers and discover how to contact them economically. In writing its profiles the management members concerned recorded reasons why each prospect might and should make an investment in an Ayala design. This attempt at insight into possible purchasing reasons gave the company clues as to potential benefits to prospects. In fact, the selling message evolved from this activity.

But the major strategy that the company promoted was its true and specific business activity—the ability to provide 'atmosphere' in its creations. Whether it be a grand Victorian pub, a Russian restaurant or a French snack bar, the company introduces 'personality' into the outlets it builds or renovates. So the company recognises and accepts its role within the

Belgian leisure industry. At the commencement of its marketing operation in Belgium during 1968/69 it estimated the total market in which it proposed to operate would be in the region of £20 million. Even establishing a 1% share—and the company planned to do just that in 1971/72 (and has succeeded) —would amount to a considerable export achievement for an almost new company, particularly as the product was so reminiscent of British character, in itself amounting to a permanent symbol and a promotional device at each site not only for British brewers but for British goods in general.

Within its marketing plan the company identified a number of problems it would have to face as an exporter. Even at this preliminary stage it was apparent that, once firmly established, it would be necessary to begin local manufacture—not just because delivery times would become critical as the business expanded but because transport costs would be prohibitive due to the product's bulk and the possibility of damage forcing insurance premiums up to intolerable levels. So part of its early contingency plan included the establishment of a Belgian subsidiary, to be founded when a predetermined volume of business had been reached. This happened almost immediately and so in 1971/72 Ayala Belgique was formed and in its first year of operation produced a profit of £14 000. A figure of £25 000 plus is expected in its second year, 1973/74.

Setting up a subsidiary gave the company greater control over its marketing effort. Using distributors often resulted, the management decided, in the two parties working in quite distinct ways, not always in the interests of the principal for often such distributors tend to go their own way.

Marketing through a subsidiary enabled Ayala to obtain maximum benefits. It was able to inspire greater confidence in the Belgian market with a more personal service for customers and the provision of on-the-spot maintenance and technical help. It also helped to reduce the cost of executive travel. In all, it enabled the company to provide a more detailed coverage of the market while exercising greater control and flexibility of its activities. It enabled the company to improve the amount and quality of market feedback.

When establishing the subsidiary the management team heeded the lessons learned by other exporters and set up a proper communications system between the two companies. It was considered essential to ensure the smooth operation of the selling effort as well as to help to ensure the appropriate motivation of local personnel.

Although the organisation's real marketing effort did not start until after 1968/69, the company learned a great deal from the success of its first erection, a prefabricated building in Place Plagey in Brussels, sold during British week in 1967. It was found that there is no substitute for salesmanship. 'Spending time on the ground' and 'show your face frequently' could easily be the company's mottos.

The one thing which distinguishes one company from another, apart from the calibre of its management and staff, is the choice of its marketing mix. As a small company, Ayala had no funds to spend on advertising, nor on an elaborate public relations campaign. But like any successful company, it established its priorities in terms of its chosen target area—made possible through the compilation of customer profiles—and set about providing the essentials of right product, right time, right price, right place. The prosperity of the chosen industrial segment hotels/pubs/catering was the only limiting factor in a country that was already prosperous and enjoyed an expanding economy. So the time was right, particularly as there was a clear growth path in leisure facilities. Although during its early exporting days, Ayala prices were 10% higher than any alternatives, it did have the advantage of being able to offer the prospect of a higher revenue potential as a result of its styles. Once local manufacture had been undertaken the company was in a position to offer prices 5% to 7% lower than the competition. As each job is a special, the company is able to offer infinite variation in design, although often, in practice, a package which includes a design, fabrication, manufacture, and construction of one of several standard products is common. So the price and the product were right as well. Belgium was chosen as the prime market largely due to its small geographical area, and being in the right place was a matter of fact, for communications and contacts were comparatively easy in a country of such a physical size. In fact, the company scores repeatedly in this market because it has established a real name for its attention to after-sales services, a factor often forgotten by solid-construction contractors. So the management team had managed to settle the requirements essential to successful trading. ,

It is believed that the company has succeeded because it researched the total European market and selected the best opportunity. It chose a significant strategy which appealed to its customers' customers and provided a product accordingly. It aroused interest in its products by selecting high-density population areas so that word-of-mouth and local editorial comment would build demand, and it has ensured customer satisfaction by providing local manufacture.

The company received the BNEC Certificate of Merit in 1971, was then given the full award in 1972 and completed its hat-trick by winning the Queen's Award to Industry for Export Achievement in 1972.

Index